SOME CASEWORK CONCEPTS
FOR THE
PUBLIC WELFARE WORKER

ALAN KEITH-LUCAS

SOME

CASEWORK

CONCEPTS

FOR THE

PUBLIC

WELFARE

WORKER

The University of North Carolina Press
CHAPEL HILL

Copyright © 1957 by
The University of North Carolina Press
All rights reserved
Manufactured in the United States of America
ISBN 0-8078-0725-7
Library of Congress Catalog Card Number 57-59583
First printing, November 1957
Second printing, April 1966
Third printing, November 1968
Fourth printing, October 1973

CONTENTS

SOME CASEWORK CONCEPTS
FOR THE
PUBLIC WELFARE WORKER

CHAPTER I

WRITING AND USING THE MATERIAL

THIS BOOK is the outcome of a course which, for one reason or another, was attended exclusively by practicing public welfare workers of whom only two had had any formal social work training. Officially the course was listed as Extension Course Social Work 210 or Social Casework I. The material for the course, with the exception of four "canned" cases—that is, actual cases carried by public welfare workers but not by members of the class—was cases on which the members of the class had themselves worked within the past few months. The "canned" cases were used as a starter until the class's cases could be collected, arranged and mimeographed. The method of presentation, the reasons for which are explained in the final chapter, was to have a panel of five class members answer certain prescribed questions about each case and then to throw the case open for general discussion. In all, nineteen such cases were discussed.

In the course of these discussions certain principles about casework began to be formulated. Some of these principles have been discussed in casework literature, notably in Herbert Aptekar's *Basic Concepts in Social Casework* (Chapel Hill: University of North Carolina Press, 1941). Others evolved from the material discussed, and one at least—that of "not disarming" the client—seems to be a contribution of this particular class to casework terminology.

I realize fully that the conceptual framework here presented is not, in fact, an "approved classification" and that many other words could be used to convey the same or similar meanings. It is, however, a framework which proved useful in a particular setting and provided the class with something of a medium for the exchange of ideas.

After the class was over, several of the students expressed the conviction that they had, in participating in the discussions, understood a number of basic principles which they believed to be "simple, practical and down-to-earth" and which were of present help to them both in evaluating their own progress as welfare workers and in giving them something to work on in the future. Several expressed the wish that these could be made available to other workers in the field.

To do exactly this would be impossible. Only actual participation in such a discussion and relating it to one's own work can carry this kind of conviction. Nevertheless, it has been done as well as I know how to do it. It should be clear, however, that this is not a comprehensive exposition of social casework, or even of social casework in a public welfare setting. It is simply a résumé of what one group of public welfare workers found it profitable to discuss in twelve two-hour sessions and what they would like to share with their co-workers and with other interested people.

The use that can be made of material of this kind will vary, of course, with the purpose for which it is used and the relationship of the user to the public welfare field. While it has been suggested by those who have read it in manuscript that it may be of use to board members, to the interested public who may want to know more of what casework "is about" and even to the more experienced worker who could do with a "refresher course" in the principles of casework, it may be of most use to those preparing for the field, to those responsible for staff training courses or practitioner courses in a school of social work, and, first and foremost, to welfare workers themselves.

How can the welfare worker who does not have professional training make use of material such as this? Not, I think, as an easy reference to some of casework's conceptualization or as a substitute for formal professional learning. For those in the field this is a "test-book," not a textbook. The important question for the practicing worker is not "Do I understand the concept of empathy (or ambivalence, or purposiveness)?" It is rather "Does my work reflect the self-discipline and understanding that is discussed here? If not, how can I better matters?" I would suggest, in fact, that workers either alone or in groups might want to select one or more of the admittedly overlapping concepts presented and test their own work against the principles set forth. Only as each idea means something in practice can it be said to be learned.

I should like to thank a number of people who read the book in manuscript and made many useful suggestions. These include, from the Bureau of Public Assistance, Miss Thomasine Hendricks, Mrs. Corinne Wolfe and Mr. George Narensky; the Commissioner of one and the Staff Training Consultants of three state departments of public welfare, Dr. Ellen Winston, Miss Ellen Bush, Mr. Curtis Ezell and Mrs. Elizabeth de Schweinitz; two local welfare superintendents, Mrs. Sarah Inman of

York County, South Carolina, and Mr. Albert King of Iredell County, North Carolina; a welfare worker, Mrs. Inez Reed of Camden, South Carolina, three teachers of social work, Miss Mary Taylor of the University of Michigan and Dr. Arthur Fink and Mr. Everett Wilson of the University of North Carolina School of Social Work; a teacher of sociology and undergraduate social work, Dr. David Stafford of Guilford College, and two of my own students in an undergraduate course, Miss Eleanor Smith and Miss Marcia Smith.

It in no way detracts from the valuable help all these have given me to say that my deepest indebtedness must be to the students in the course. No one can teach such a course without learning a lot himself, and no such course is possible without the wholehearted engagement in it of its students. In a very real sense this book is dedicated to and owes more than I can express to the welfare workers of the two Carolinas whose enthusiasm, devotion to their jobs, willingness to engage in self-criticism and basic integrity, as well as their practical knowledge and sound common sense, transformed what might have been a time-consuming chore into a most heartening and, indeed, exciting experience.

CHAPTER II

WHAT DO WE MEAN BY CASEWORK?

WHAT DO WE MEAN by the word "casework"? If one asks this of a group of public welfare workers one gets all sorts of answers. To some the word has come to mean something that good public welfare workers, and especially those who have been to a school of social work, do or would like to do over and above certifying Mrs. A. for a grant or getting Mr. B. to a hospital—something intangible, rarefied and somewhat mysterious for which there is never enough time, but which, if given, will somehow cause clients to want to be independent or stop quarrelling with their wives. To others it seems to mean being always ready with the appropriate service for an individual client's needs—vocational rehabilitation, psychiatric care, a foster home—anything as long as it isn't public assistance which isn't casework at all. People are apt to talk about something called "casework services" which can be counted and are, in their opinion, the only "real" job of the public welfare agency despite its rather routine duty also to provide public assistance grants.

This is not at all what I, or this book, or indeed many other people, mean by "casework." Casework, as the word is used here, is simply the way in which the agency, through its workers—or the worker, in the name of the agency—makes available a service which the agency is empowered to give. This service may be public assistance. As a matter of fact, it often is, since money is a very important factor in our civilization. But it can also be any number of other things, such as arranging for medical care, or supplying a foster home, or providing a way in which a delinquent child can stay at home through the use of probation, or help in filling out a social security form, or making available the particular and sometimes rather complicated service known as "counselling."

There is no particular reason for us to try to establish which of these many services is the most important or requires the greatest amount of knowledge and experience to administer. The point is that we have, or may have, responsibility to make any or all of them available to a client who may see in them some hope of a solution, or some step toward a solution, of whatever it is that has made him so uncomfortable that he has asked for our help. Our job is to help him find out whether indeed the service we offer is in fact helpful to him and to help him use it if he can.

We can do this badly or well. If we offer him the service casually, or impulsively, or indulgently, or hatefully or thoughtlessly—if, by the way in which the service is offered or given, he remains as confused, as fearful, as unable to care for himself or to make his own decisions as he was before (or, as sometimes happens, even more so)—then the probability is that we have not done very good casework. There are, of course, some people who cannot use any service to which we have access, but in these cases we at least need to consider whether we have really done all we could to make our services work. If, on the other hand, our service has been offered or given thoughtfully, responsibly and understandingly—if the client has gained from it some little bit of increased courage, some little ability that he didn't have before to make decisions for himself, some small measure of contentment or enjoyment of life—then our casework has been good.

This change inside the person who is asking for help can come in many different ways. It can also come as the result of the way that any service is given—as surely and as completely in public assistance as in a more intangible service. Because it must have a name by which we can refer to it I am going to call it "movement." It is, in one sense, the goal of casework—that is, good casework makes movement possible. In another sense it cannot be a goal since, as we shall see, a caseworker cannot decide or even predict what kind of movement shall or should take place. He can only provide conditions in which it can grow if it will.

CHAPTER III

THE IDEA OF MOVEMENT

MOVEMENT, in the casework sense, means taking hold of one's problem, doing something about it, not sitting down under it. It is getting one's foot on the ladder. It doesn't necessarily mean doing what we, or society, or anyone else thinks is the right thing to do, because one of the characteristics of movement is that it is full of trial and error, that it sometimes involves the person in what looks like a backward move before a forward move is possible. Perhaps we can understand this if we think of a person who has lived all his life in darkness and silence. If he should suddenly find a way to hear and see he will make many mistakes at first. He may do many apparently stupid things but all the same he will have gained something very valuable to him, and in time things will straighten out. Or we could imagine a person who is tightly bound. In bursting out of his bonds he may do a certain amount of damage, but he will be free.

Movement, of course, is rarely as dramatic as this, although sometimes it actually is so. Often it looks to us like a very little step but one which, if we examine it, is really the first step on the ladder.

In the following case the movement may look slight indeed:

Willie Horne, fifty-nine, was brought to the office to make application for assistance by Mr. Edward Cantey. Mr. Cantey stated that he had known Willie for several years, that he was a good, deserving person and now was sick and needed help. Mr. Cantey took entire charge of the conversation, giving Willie no opportunity. Willie sat quietly, hands hanging between knees, saying nothing. He appeared mentally slow, had a cocked eye and the other had a queer expression. He volunteered no information, and worker had to pull out information regarding his present situation to supplement that given by Mr. Cantey.

This continued until worker asked Willie if he had any way of establishing his age.

Mr. Cantey laughed and said he knew he had none. Worker asked Willie if he had a Social Security card or a Registration card. All men had to register for the armed services during the Second World War. Willie immediately showed more interest and rooted around in his pocket and produced both of them. He proudly handed them over to worker. It was noticed that both were in the name of Willie Holmes. Upon being questioned about this Willie sat up straight and said he did not know why people called him Horne for his name was Holmes and always had been. Mr. Cantey was completely surprised and said he had never known this before. Worker told Willie that of course the application would be taken in his correct name and he would be known by this to the worker. Willie smiled for the first time during interview and started talking. He said that he had always worked hard, mostly at the Buffalo Oil Mill. Later, when he had had to give this up he had done work in yards for ladies around town. The money from a grandson had been a big help. He gave all other information necessary for completing forms for application like a changed person. Worker gave him the medical form to take to doctor and added a note asking for his visual acuity as some service may be rendered there.

* * * * * * * * * * * * *

Willie thanked worker as well as Mr. Cantey before leaving. He was holding his cards proudly in his hand when he left.

Yet this is really no small change. A man, it might be said, has a new outlook on life, a new pride, a new resolution, and this the worker enabled to grow by the simple means of recognizing him as Willie Holmes, the man who has a right to his own name, rather than as Willie Horne, Mr. Cantey's protegée.

In another case brought to class a man who had been very fearful of vocational rehabilitation and what it would involve ends a contact by coming to the office to get the vocational rehabilitation counsellor's address. Although "still in a doubtful mood" and "wanting assurance" of the agency's support he has brought with him the list of tools he will need and a stamped envelope—a small indication, perhaps, but a very real and practical one.

In still a third case movement comes as a result of the client's blazing anger at having been rejected for public assistance, out of which she fashions the courage to cut herself free from the relatives on whom she has been unwillingly dependent and to strike out on her own.

A second important characteristic of movement is that it is something that happens inside the client. It is something he really means, believes

in, does of his own will. It is not something into which he has been
cajoled, threatened, flattered, persuaded or trapped. We may mistake
this for movement, but in time we will find out that it is not.

Consider the case, for instance, of a man who was suffering from a
fairly extensive hernia which prevented him from following his normal
occupation in a warehouse. Considering himself incapacitated he applied
for public assistance. The medical review team which had to pass on
his case considered the hernia reparable. The worker goes to discuss
with him the findings of this team.

Worker told Mr. Paynter that she had good news for him. The medical
review team believed that he could have his hernia repaired and the department could arrange for this at no cost to Mr. Paynter. Worker gave Mr.
Paynter an appointment to see Dr. Barnes the following Tuesday at 9 A.M. and
asked him to be sure to keep the appointment.

Mr. Paynter said that he did not believe that the hernia could be repaired.
He was too old for that sort of thing. Worker told him that the doctors were
very hopeful in his case and that we had also discussed his case with the V.R.
Counsellor who had said that there was plenty of work available for a man
of his experience. Mr. Paynter said that he would surely like to get back to
work again and began to tell again how he and his family had suffered since
he had been sick. Worker told him that she thought his troubles would soon
be over and mentioned that he could receive public assistance until the outcome of the operation was known.

Mr. Paynter was asked if he had any fears about the operation and said
that he did not. He was concerned about getting to Dr. Barnes's on time since
he did not have any transportation. Worker offered to carry him to the doctor
since she had to be in that territory that day. Mr. Paynter added that he had
a bad cold and perhaps Dr. Barnes would prefer to see him when he was
better. Worker thought Dr. Barnes would want to see him in any case and
asked Mr. Paynter if he did not want to get well as soon as possible. Mr.
Paynter agreed that he did and thanked worker effusively for her help.

It might look as if Mr. Paynter was "showing movement." He *did*
go to the doctor. He *did* undergo the operation. He *did,* with the help
of the Vocational Rehabilitation Counsellor, find himself a new job, in
the same warehouse, where he did not have to lift heavy bundles. But
this, good as it seemed, was an illusory movement. Within three months
Mr. Paynter was sick again, this time with a form of asthma that effectually prevented his working.

What went wrong? We cannot tell, exactly. What we do know is
this—that Mr. Paynter had a problem much deeper than an unrepaired
hernia. Perhaps it was a gnawing fear that he really couldn't compete
with other, stronger men in his job, or perhaps, after his injury, he found

that his greatest pride—his masculine strength—was gone and that to take a more "sissy" job seemed to him like defeat. The only movement that would have been real would have been to face this feeling or fear and do something about it.

But this the caseworker would not let him do. When he tried to express his doubts she swept them aside. She made it impossible for him even to express them—didn't he want to get well? She had her own idea of what his movement should be. He should get himself to the doctor. And Mr. Paynter gave in. He went along with the worker, perhaps persuading himself for the moment that she was right and at any rate not daring to seem to deny her wishes for him. Only the movement was hers, not his, and in the end it proved its uselessness for him. His body revolted—it should perhaps be explained here that asthma is often, but not always, a way in which the body expresses a mental strain that is too hard to bear.

And yet the worker sincerely thought that she was helping Mr. Paynter become independent again. She made the mistake that so many of us are prone to make. In her desire to see movement she forgot that the only true movement comes from the inside. It cannot be hurried, or induced by the worker, from outside.

Some movement, of course, takes place whenever a client takes the step of getting himself to an agency. It is our job to see that this movement is allowed or encouraged to continue. This is sometimes difficult because we haven't thought through what it has meant to the client to take this first step and because the client often wraps up his fear or his anger at having to do this by being demanding, or whiny, or bitter or apparently self-satisfied. The movement doesn't feel good to us. We don't recognize it as part of the client's way of battling his way out of his difficulty. We try to choke it off, or we choke it off without thinking.

Consider Mrs. Farmer, for instance:

Mrs. Farmer, a rather tight-lipped, bony woman in her early fifties, was in the office with her granddaughter, Eva Kate, thirteen. I noticed the two sitting on opposite sides of the waiting room while I saw my previous appointment. Eva Kate was thin and unattractive with straight lank hair and a dress at least four inches too long for her by modern standards. Mrs. Farmer sat in silence until I came for her. When I did she turned to Eva Kate and told her, "You stay there till this is through. Do you hear?" Eva Kate didn't answer. I said to Mrs. F. that she had had a long wait. Her lips clamped down all the more tightly as she brushed this aside, and she said belligerently, "I want what's coming to me. You're giving Mrs. Hill thirty dollars a month for her granddaughter. What will you give me for Eva Kate?"

We all know that public assistance is not given like that. In fact some of us may feel that we spend half our lives explaining just this. We may also guess—and we would be right—that Mrs. Farmer is not actually in financial need, that her trouble lies deeper than that. As a matter of fact when she and the worker get down to discussing a budget and Mrs. Farmer is asked, item by item, what she is willing to contribute to Eva Kate's support (which is the way ADC with a relative is working in the state in question) Mrs. Farmer can't say that she doesn't want to contribute anything but Eva Kate's clothes and some toilet incidentals. It also seems that she and Mr. Farmer are better off than they were when they first took Eva Kate four years ago. Quite obviously the real problem is one of relationship, and Mrs. Farmer indicates this indirectly. After some discussion of how hard it must be for Mrs. Farmer to find the program what it is and not what she had hoped it would be:

Mrs. Farmer said that this is all the thanks she gets for caring for her granddaughter. Not that she doesn't love the child or would dream of not doing her best for her, but she doesn't feel that she and her husband should have to put out their own money, little as it was, to support the child just because her daughter's husband turned out to be "no good." She said she had warned her daughter not to marry the man. He was a foreigner, an Italian, she said, and not even a decent Christian. She described with a great deal of feeling the interview she had with her daughter immediately after the runaway marriage. Mrs. F. was quite bitter about her daughter's hard-headedness and some of the things she had said.

After the caseworker has helped her come back to Eva Kate and her problems:

Mrs. Farmer told me of her son-in-law's death and how, soon after, the daughter had contracted TB and gone to a sanatorium. Eva Kate was eight or nine. They had taken her in—what else could they do?—even though Mr. Farmer had been unemployed at the time. She hoped that they would never have to go through that kind of hard times again. It was hard sledding, but they had managed somehow. They hadn't had room, really. Eva Kate had had to sleep in the same bedroom as Mr. and Mrs. F. That wasn't so bad as it had become lately when Eva Kate had begun to want to stay out at night. Mr. and Mrs. F. always go to bed early. They're up early, too, not like some people. Mrs. F. closed her mouth firmly.

I said that it seemed to me that Mrs. F. was saying that things were near a breaking point. Mrs. F. said grimly, "I told that young woman that if she weren't in by nine, I'd have her grandfather take his belt to her. The little snip. She knows she could twist her granpa 'round her little finger. He never raised his hand to either of our own girls. Nor did I. Though maybe I should have. If I had, maybe Evie Belle wouldn't have done what she did."

Mrs. Farmer has many problems. One can see her feeling about her own daughter, her feeling of lack of support from her husband, her apparent inability to understand the normal behavior of an adolescent. One wonders how she can begin to move with all this on her. Yet she does move in the interview. Curiously enough this is not in the area of what we might think of as her real problem—getting direct help in thinking through her relationship with Eva Kate. She is offered the chance to move here but she cannot. Having told the caseworker all this she stops. "Why should I tell you all this?" I said I didn't know; maybe she felt it was important. She said shortly, no, it wasn't. How about money for Eva Kate?

And yet, of course, money is not what will help Mrs. Farmer. There is, in fact, evidence that the getting of ADC would mean to her only that she could force someone else to take part of the responsibility for this difficult granddaughter who reminds her of her failure with her daughter. And it is characteristically in her failure to get this money—a failure to which she herself contributes because at the bottom of her heart she wants to be responsible for Eva Kate—that she finds strength.

This strength—this movement—is simply the realization that Eva Kate is her responsibility, that she cannot side-step or duck the problem.

This results, a few days later, in what may look like a very backward piece of movement. Eva Kate comes in late one night. Mrs. Farmer, holding to her new resolution, does something about it. What in fact she does is to march Eva Kate down to the cellar and whale her with the carpet-beater. This lands her into deeper trouble, but at the same time it begins to clarify the problem. Mr. Farmer cries more than Eva Kate; that young lady becomes openly defiant and threatens to run to her mother, forcing Mrs. Farmer to admit that the daughter is in town and that the fear of Eva Kate's doing just this is one of the things that has prevented her coming to terms with the child. Mrs. Farmer considers reform school but rejects it. She wants the caseworker to talk to Eva Kate. This the caseworker will do only under certain conditions:

I said that I could see Eva Kate, but I thought that we might consider a little what would be involved. I couldn't take over Mrs. Farmer's job of disciplining her granddaughter. Mrs. Farmer nodded. That meant that I couldn't be used as a punishment. Eva Kate would have to trust me, and that would mean that she'd have to be sure that she could tell me how she felt in confidence. I emphasized the last words. Mrs. Farmer said, "You mean you would not tell me." I said that I couldn't promise to tell her all that Eva Kate said, and Eva Kate would need to know it, just as she would have to know that I wouldn't permit her to tell me of plans that would be really dangerous to her, such as running away, without letting Mrs. Farmer know. But I'd have to let her tell me about how she felt about Mrs. Farmer, if I was to be of any help. Mrs. Farmer sat in silence. Then with a wry little smile she said, "That was quite a licking I gave her." I said I might have to go further and discuss with Eva Kate her feelings about her mother.

Mrs. Farmer said, "I think she's seeing her mother. That's what I'm afraid of. It wasn't true what I told you. Evie Belle did have TB but she's been out for a year or more. They tell me she's in town." She turned on me, suddenly a little angry. "You think I ought to let her see Eva Kate, don't you?" I said that I'd have no way of saying yes or no to that. All I could say at the moment was that Mrs. Farmer didn't seem sure that she could be a complete mother to Eva Kate. Eva Kate wouldn't let her, nor would Mr. Farmer, and Mrs. F. was reaching out for someone to take over some or all of the job. Mrs. Farmer nodded. "He thinks I was too hard on her. I think he's been seeing her too." I said that this must feel very much as if everyone were against her. Mrs. Farmer said very quietly, "If only she'd come to me. I'm her mother." She thought for a minute and then said softly, and with quite a new expression, "I'm not hard-hearted, really. Only hard-headed, I declare."

The climax comes two weeks later.

I happened to meet Mrs. Farmer, Eva Kate, and Eva Kate's mother on the street. Eva Kate was wearing a much more suitable dress which made her look much younger. She introduced me to her mother, who was a pretty, rather shallow-looking young woman. Eva Kate explained that her mother was leaving shortly for a job on the coast. "I'm going to stay with Gran for a while." Mrs. F. said, with a little smile, that that depended on how long Eva Kate could put up with her granny's and grandfather's old-fashioned ways.

There has certainly been movement in this case. It has not come all at once. It has been a backward and forward movement, and at one time it looked as if Mrs. Farmer was going to spoil everything, but in the end she found in the experience the courage to allow her love for her daughter and her granddaughter to overcome her pride and guilt. One thing that might be noted about this case, too, is that in a sense the agency has not given Mrs. Farmer any actual "service." In turn she and the agency have discussed public assistance, referral to Girl's Industrial School and a counselling service for Eva Kate. None of these were the answer to Mrs. Farmer's need. It was, in fact, in Mrs. Farmer's discovery that these services carried with them certain conditions and responsibilities on her part that she could not meet that she discovered her own responsibility.

Now, then, did the worker help Mrs. Farmer? Part of the help was provided by the policies of the agency, by these very conditions and responsibilities it put around its services, but the real motive force was the way that the caseworker carried out her job. It may seem a little at this time as if what she did was somewhat magical, but actually she knew what she was doing all the time. Some of the principles on which her work and the work of any successful caseworker can be guided are discussed in the following chapters.

CHAPTER IV

UNDERSTANDING AMBIVALENCE

PUBLIC WELFARE WORKERS are often baffled by clients who do nothing about their own situation. The worker works hard on their behalf, Referrals are made to jobs, or hospitals, or recreational facilities and the client never follows through, even when it is obvious to the meanest intelligence that it is to his advantage to do so. The community, and sometimes the welfare worker, too, thinks of the client as "no-count" or lazy or stupid or lacking in ambition. Often the community wants to punish these people by cutting them off assistance. The welfare worker, more humane but perhaps not any more understanding, often resorts to persuasion, "urging," praise or blame. In how many records does one not read, "Worker has urged Mr. C. repeatedly to do so-and-so but for some reason he has never been able to do it"?

What is this force that prevents people from moving when all common sense suggests that they should, even when they know that the results of not moving will be disastrous to themselves? Is it actually a defect in the character? If so, there may not be too much we can do to help. I would like to suggest that in most cases what we are up against is a phenomenon known as ambivalence.

Ambivalence simply means that in every desire to do something there is also a desire not to do it; that every positive feeling also has in it something of the negative. We all know this to be true in lesser ways. You may enjoy reading this material—I hope that you do—but at the same time it is taking you away from something else which you want, or ought, to do. Or maybe, having just read the Farmer case, it has made you a little critical of your own practice or more than a little mad at the writer who won't explain all at once what the worker did or at the worker with whom you disagree because you would never have let Mrs. Farmer spank Eva Kate and get away with it. If these negative feelings outweigh the positive ones you will put the book down. We are also aware that emotions and their opposites or seeming opposites are often very close together—"I hate you because I love you. I love you because I hate you." Incidentally, the real opposite of love is not hate. It is indifference.

In most situations, however, one side of our emotions or desires far outweighs the other. It is when it doesn't, when our desire to do something is almost equally balanced by a desire not to do it, or a fear of doing it, that we are in trouble. We actually say, "I don't know which way to turn." And this is the situation in which many of our clients find themselves. After all, it isn't pleasant having to ask for help. It isn't pleasant to have to tell a stranger all about ourselves and our affairs. It isn't pleasant—although to some people it may be a lesser evil—to be dependent on someone else. It does mean confessing somewhere, to one's self or to others, that one is a failure, and this is just as true whether or not we cover up this fear by being demanding or aggressive or by complaining. In fact it is because of this fear that clients behave like that.

Mr. Paynter, who developed a new sickness after his hernia was repaired, was ambivalent. He wanted to work and yet he feared to. Mrs. Farmer was ambivalent. She both loved Eva Kate and wanted to punish her, even to get rid of her. She both loved her daughter, Evie Belle, and disapproved of her. She both wanted help and didn't want to undertake the responsibilities it entailed. She may or may not have actually known it so that she could put it into words. In one case brought to the class, for instance, a mother was complaining about her husband who had attacked her physically.

What sort of help do you think he needs, Mrs. Hump? "I think he needs to get away from us until his mind gets settled. Someone told me about a place up near Du Pont. Now it's not the 'Crazy House' but a place where they help people to get their minds settled." I then asked, What does his doctor advise? "I don't know, I want you to call him and tell him that something's got to be done—that me and my children just can't go on living this way (she sobs again), but I would like for him to go to this home for treatment."

Perhaps he should go someplace for treatment, but we will have to discuss this with him and also his doctor—but, how do you plan to take care of the expenses involved in this sort of plan?

"I talked with the man from the Heart Association and he said that he would try to work out something for Harold to do. They mentioned his raising parakeets—but I told him he couldn't do that at home because Bob has asthma so bad. He was to let him know something in two weeks, but I still haven't heard anything."

At the same time that she is considering placing her husband in a mental hospital she is concerned about her inability to proceed with a plan for him to work at home.

Sometimes ambivalence is very hard to see. The counter-feeling is felt to be shameful and is hidden away, as Mr. Paynter hid from the worker his fears about work, because he knew that she would disapprove of them. It helps, however, if we remember that ambivalence is always present, in greater or lesser degree, in any human activity.

How, then, do we help an ambivalent person? One of the workers in the class brought in the following interview, held with a man who had been referred to vocational rehabilitation after it had been determined medically that his apparent heart condition was psychosomatic—that is, due to his nervous condition rather than to any damage to his heart.

Mr. Wallace in agency office to keep an appointment with V. R. Counselor, then asked to see the worker. Mr. Wallace began to explain plans made with V. R. to open an auto repair shop. Worker felt there was a very noticeable lack of enthusiasm or interest on the part of Mr. Wallace regarding the plans made with V. R. With a great rush of words, Mr. Wallace began to relate that he doubted if he would ever be able to work enough to provide for his family. He repeatedly said he could hardly get his breath and was afraid he had a bad heart.

Worker explained to Mr. Wallace that the agency was interested, not only in providing financial assistance during the period of his disability, but also in offering our help to him in understanding and using any services that we had that he felt would be helpful to him in moving toward rehabilitation. Worker wondered if Mr. Wallace were interested in working with V. R. because he felt it was an eligibility requirement, or if he felt there was a fair chance of his resuming his role of provider for his family.

Mr. Wallace stated that he did not have much hope of ever again being able to be the sole support for his family, but he hated to ask Department of Public Welfare for a dime, and that in talking with the V. R. man he was clutching at the only slim chance that seemed available to him. Worker explained to Mr. Wallace that we could understand his desire to be self-sufficient and that we were quite willing to provide any available service that would enable him to again get on his feet, but at the same time we wanted him to understand that if his step forward in setting up an auto repair business were too difficult for him physically or provided insufficient funds for his family the ADC grant would be available according to regulations. Mr. Wallace said, "You mean by that if I go to work you won't cut off my check?" Worker explained the budget would be worked out with him and if his income was not enough to meet the needs of his family he could still get a grant until his earnings were enough to meet his needs. Mr. Wallace asked, "What if I do make enough to support my family, then get sick?" Worker explained he could be reinstated for the ADC payment if he was not able to work and his family was in need. Mr. Wallace said he would like to think awhile about opening a shop for he did not know if he would be able to do the work. Worker told him he would be his own boss and could work as he felt like it or could stop and rest awhile anytime he wanted to, or when he felt he needed to rest. Mr. Wallace said he would not say today what he would do as he wanted to think about the shop awhile.

Mr. Wallace came back once more the same day, full of questions and doubts, before the triumphant conclusion, mentioned in the previous chapter, in which he brought into the office his list of tools and a stamped envelope.

When this case was presented to the class the majority of the panel didn't like it. They felt that the worker was in some way encouraging Mr. Wallace to fail, that she was giving him an easy "out." In part I think this was due to the philosophy in our culture which calls on us to "accentuate the positive, eliminate the negative." The man who wrote this phrase, however, was no caseworker. If we examine the case more closely we can see that it was only because the worker recognized Mr. Wallace's ambivalence and reassured him that failure to make good (which was, in essence, what he feared) would not mean actual disaster that he found the courage to go forward. There are other things, too, in the worker's handling which were helpful and which we will take up later, but this is the central point. If, for instance, you were to be promoted to supervisor and were unsure of your ability to do the work, would you be most likely to accept the challenge if you knew that if you failed you could have your old job back, or if you knew that taking the new job would mean "burning your boats?"

The natural reaction of a worker faced with ambivalence is to urge the client in one way or another, to trot out the advantages of doing something. In a few cases, where the only problem is that the client hasn't actually ever seen the advantages in a course of action, this may work. But it is not usually lack of knowledge that holds a person back. Often neighbors and friends have long given him the benefit of their advice. What holds people back is fear. If the worker had spent her time encouraging Mr. Wallace to accept vocational rehabilitation all she would have done would have been to make his fear less and less admissible but all the stronger.

The recognition of negatives is important even where the client does not have a choice. Some welfare workers for instance, have the responsibility of enforcing school attendance laws. Here is a worker talking to a boy who has quit school illegally and assumed the father role in the family to provide, chiefly, medical care for his mother:

Worker began by telling Alvin that she had heard very nice things about him. She thought it was very fine of him to work and give up his chances for a good education in order to help his mother. She was glad to be able to tell him that this would not be necessary in future. The family would be receiving an ADC check of about $70.00 a month. While this was not as much as he made by working, it would enable him to return to school, and worker was sure he could pick up odd jobs after school, and even work in vacation time, to add to the family income. Alvin said that he did not want to go back to school. He would fail the tenth grade because of his long absence. Worker said she would clear with the principal, but she was almost certain that this was not so, as Alvin was such an excellent pupil. Alvin said he didn't think school would do him much good, anyway. He had already been promised much better jobs than the one he had. Worker tried to get him to see that with a high school education he would have a much wider choice of jobs. She knew that he wanted to look after his mother and by going to school now he could make himself much more able to do so in the future.

Alvin returned to school, all right, for a period of seven days. At the end of this time he took his father's gun and took himself out of the state. When last heard of he was heading for Texas.

What could the worker have done? She could have recognized with Alvin that he did not want to go back to school—that he had enjoyed his independence and grown-up-ness. She could have understood his anxiety for his mother and the possibility that he did not trust the welfare department to take his place in meeting her needs. She could have let him know that she understood how important it was to him to be the one who met this need. Then she could have let him know that neither she nor he was free in face of the school attendance laws. He had a choice to make and only he could make it. It is possible, of course, that he would still have headed for Texas, which is what he did anyway. Even if he had—which I take the liberty to doubt—it would have been a much more considered, less impulsive choice.

CHAPTER V

EMPATHY

IN THE SUCCESSFUL CASES or bits of cases presented so far the worker has obviously done something more than just understand the client's ambivalence, important as this is. She has somehow put herself into a position in which a client can express himself and take the steps he needs to. In some way she has made it safe for the client to do so.

Let us look again for a moment at the worker in the Farmer case. Mrs. Farmer comes in with her preposterous demand for assistance. When the worker explains that there is a program that helps relatives and asks her if she wants to discuss it further her answer is, "I don't need to discuss it. Just give me the money for Eva Kate."

The worker does not argue or oppose Mrs. Farmer at this point. Indeed she says that it must be hard to ask for help and to realize that it could only be given under certain conditions. It may seem a small thing to have said but it did at least put the emphasis of the interview on what Mrs. Farmer was thinking and feeling and it did enable her actually to discuss the conditions involved instead of merely resenting them.

Similarly, when Mrs. Farmer has done the rather dreadful thing of thrashing her granddaughter the worker, who actually must have been rather shocked at Mrs. Farmer's beginning efforts at moving, responds with understanding of what to have done such a thing means to Mrs. Farmer. As Mrs. Farmer blurts out the story the worker responds: "I said that Mrs. Farmer must have been feeling pretty desperate." At this Mrs. Farmer breaks down and through her tears—real movement for this tight-lipped, rigidly controlled woman—begins to struggle with her ambivalence.

What was conveyed to Mrs. Farmer in these two instances was not what we usually mean when we use the word "sympathy." She was not sorry for Mrs. Farmer. She didn't agree with her that Eva Kate needed a licking or that conditions placed around ADC were, as Mrs. Farmer called them, "red-tape." To feel *like* a client is of little help to him in his battle to overcome the feelings that are part of his trouble. What the worker did, and let Mrs. Farmer know that she did, was to understand what these things must feel like to Mrs. Farmer. This is feeling *for* Mrs. Farmer and *with* Mrs. Farmer but not *like* her.

This feeling, which must be both genuine—insincerity is very easily detected and in any case will probably mean that the worker will mis-judge the feeling—and communicated to the client, is what we mean by empathy. It is not something that is arrived at easily. In the first place rather few of us have been hungry, confused and desperate in the same way that our clients have. We have therefore to call on reserves of imagination and the known experience of others. In the second, the client's feeling may be very distasteful to us, or even dangerous, because having to feel with our client in this way upsets some of the ways in which we have schooled ourselves to feel. Thus the worker who listened to Mrs. Farmer's description of beating Eva Kate had to overcome her natural revulsion at such a harsh way of treating an obviously misunder-stood and deprived teen-ager who had asked, pathetically, as her grand-mother came out of the first interview: "Well, will they pay you to keep me?" She may also have had to struggle with her own feelings when, perhaps, she was herself spanked as a child and this seemed an intolerable invasion of her own privacy or self-respect. Still further, she may have had to repress her own anger with her own children, so that to be pleasant to a child-beater may have felt like a betrayal or like playing with fire. Notice, however, that the worker did not have to change or betray her feelings about this type of punishment. She did not have to agree with Mrs. Farmer. What she had to do was to discipline her feeling, to keep her focus not on what she herself felt but on what she could feel for and with her unhappy client.

Again, the client's feeling may be directed towards us, or our agency, or the program in which we have a stake. Thus a worker who ap-proached a mother about complaints that had been received about the care of a child had to make use of this disciplined feeling. Here he was, partly concerned about the child, who sounded as if she might be seriously malnourished, and partly very reluctant to intrude on this family and bring to them the implied threat of court action. Having helped the mother first admit him, then turn her anger from unproductive anger towards the complainant to anger at him, and finally to a readiness to discuss the complaint, he is faced with the question: "What are they say-ing about Patsy?"

I detailed the complaints. She said it was not true about the gas, which had been turned on yesterday. I said that must have made it much easier; it must be hard to feed a child properly without gas. There was some softening in Mrs. H.'s expression, but she did not answer me. After a while when I looked up, I noticed that she was crying gently. I said, "Has it been very hard?"

She began to tell me about how hard it had been. She described their hopes of getting on their feet again, but that something always seemed to go wrong. She said nothing about any marital difficulty and specifically did not blame her husband. She said that in the last three weeks her brother had died. She had had an eviction notice and now . . . and she looked at me. I said I realized that my coming was probably almost the last straw.

It was this recognition that enabled the mother to bring out her real fears about what was happening to her child and to discuss them with a worker who now she knew could understand and whom, ten minutes later, she was able to ask for help in getting the counselling service she needed.

Yet this was not easy for the worker to do. He had got into the home; he was beginning to have some sort of superficially pleasant relationship with the client. He might so easily have thought it unnecessary to bring up again the threat that he represented to the family. And yet he knew that this threat had not actually been resolved. He must not be defensive about it and deny or ignore his client's feeling about it.

On a somewhat simpler level either lack of empathy or an inability to convey it seems to have stymied the worker's efforts to help in a case brought in to class in which an unmarried girl with two illegitimate children is the only one—her mother having died very recently—to care for a bedridden father.

Home visit made for purpose of periodic review of Mr. Holland's OAA grant.

Worker met at door by Jane, a very pretty girl who gave the appearance of a rather depressed and lifeless person. Mr. Holland still in bed. (Details of his condition and budget discussion at this point omitted.) Jane answered most of worker's questions and furnished practically all information about father and family's situation. She stated since Mrs. Holland's death she must remain at home to care for her father and new baby. The only income for the family is Mr. Holland's OAA check of $45.00. Jane told worker they would be unable to live off this amount during the winter months. Worker asked what Jane's plans were. She stated she had none. Worker explained that Jane could be included in father's budget as an essential person in the home but this could not pass the $54.00 maximum. Jane stated she understood this but they could not make ends meet on this amount. Worker said the

Department of Public Welfare did have a program in which we helped mothers but it did involve certain responsibilities and obligations on her part—in this case it would mean involving the father. Worker then asked about the children's father—had he helped any or would he be willing to? Jane said no in a manner closing the conversation.

Worker commented on what a fine baby she had and that she would like to meet her other boy. Jane smiled for the first time and seemed very proud of baby. Conversation was about baby for a while and during this worker felt a small amount of contact was made. Worker then asked if Jane knew of the ADC program, explaining necessity of warrant against the father. She said yes she understood and really needed the money. Worker explained how community set up regulations for giving assistance. Could she accept the fact that she had a responsibility in accepting aid? No answer from Jane. Worker then asked did she see the children's father having any responsibility? Could she talk with worker regarding her feelings for children and their father? A very vague and meaningless answer. Worker asked if she were willing to take out a warrant. Jane was rather uncertain. All through discussion Jane was very agreeable toward worker and repeatedly expressed need of money. Worker explained again that there is certain information we need to have and certain requirements to be met before assistance could be given. Perhaps she was saying to me that her relationship with her friend was more important than money for her children. No comment from Jane. Worker then said we were willing to work with her but she must be willing to involve herself in working through her problem. She said she would contact worker in next few days regarding her decision.

The worker here recognizes Jane's ambivalence although not perhaps the depth of it—it certainly looks most unrealistic for Jane not to apply for ADC. (In this case a little more understanding of the unmarried mother might have been helpful. Often the father is a very unreal person in her life. In fact one member of the class told of an unmarried mother who, when faced with the requirement of trying to obtain help from him, gasped, horrified, "But, ma'am, I don't know him well enough for that.") The worker is also very pleasant and she implicitly "forgives" Jane for her behavior by praising the baby and by asking to meet the older child. But nowhere is there any indication that the worker has empathy for Jane in her feelings at having been left suddenly responsible through her mother's death, in her feelings about this death, in her struggle between her duty to her father and her need to be independent, or in her fears about her marital situation. One can be pretty sure that some or all of these things were weighing on Jane but that she cannot risk talking about them until she knows that the caseworker knows something of her feelings and will not blame her. The result is that Jane doesn't talk and doesn't move and the worker comes away with a self-confessed sense of failure.

Empathy is also missing in the beginning passages of a tape-recorded interview brought to class, despite the conventional sympathy shown over the loss of a son:

CW: Good morning, Mr. P——. How are you today? I am A—— B——, the Revolving Worker.

Mr. P., our conversation is going to be recorded over the microphone in order that I might get all the information that both you and I say, and when we talk, if we will just talk over the table, the microphone will pick up our voices and record what is being said. Mrs. Broom, our receptionist, tells me that you wish to make application for Old Age Assistance. I have your old record here. Now, is your wife Molly Ruff Putman?

Mr. P.: Mabel.

CW: You have three children?

Mr. P.: Just two now, the boy is dead. He died three weeks ago.

CW: He died three weeks ago? Which one? Edward? What was the trouble? I'm so sorry to hear about his death.

Mr. P.: A blood clot on his lung, I think. They have a big name for it, but I can't tell you what it was.

*CW: Could you tell me a little about yourself, Mr. P.?

Mr. P.: Well, I just a——, I'm not able to work, or earn a decent living. I figured I had attained the age and uh, I thought I would see if I could get some help from the Welfare.

CW: How old are you, Mr. P.?

Mr. P.: 68, May past.

*CW: 68, May past? What do you do for a living, Mr. P.?

Mr. P.: Well, I'm not doing anything much. I've tried turkeying a little and chickening a little and I didn't do any good at that.

CW: Do you have any source of income?

Several things might be noted here. One is the absence of any attempt to communicate to Mr. P. the worker's understanding of his possible discomfort at asking for assistance or his feeling about the microphone. Another is the use of a professionalized and rather puzzling title. (I would as soon meet a Whirling Dervish as a Revolving Worker.) A third is the way in which the caseworker somewhat relentlessly pursues his own need for information without having come to terms with what Mr. P.'s statements mean or what he is feeling. This results in several abrupt changes of subject, two of which are marked by asterisks in the text. The same type of interviewing continues through twenty-two questions by the caseworker and twenty-two answers by Mr. P. The caseworker then plunges into a description of Old Age Assistance which takes nearly five minutes and into which Mr. P. has finally to break with the question that seems to be bothering him all along—the possibility of his wife's getting assistance in her own right, something that might, in fact, have been discovered much earlier when Mr. P. is indignant that his wife does not receive social security. It is scarcely surprising that at the end of the interview Mr. P. does not know whether or not he wants assistance. Whatever he feels about his situation, or public assistance, or his wife, the caseworker never explores with him. He is too busy investigating the man's eligibility for a public assistance the client does not understand to meet him even halfway in his feeling. In justice to the worker I feel that I ought to say, however, that a tape recording is a very severe test of an interview and that sometimes empathy can be conveyed by tone of voice and gesture that does not appear in print.

Empathy should not be mistaken for softness or indulgence. Welfare workers are often accused of being soft. Sometimes, of course, they are, but when they are they are using sympathy, not empathy. Empathy, in fact, sometimes hurts. The client wants to forget or deny that he is feeling as he is. Mrs. Farmer broke down and cried at the worker's empathy. Thus in one case brought into class a worker had provided ADC most sympathetically for a family who were clearly neglecting their children; when the police acted and the children were removed he most sympathetically found a house for the mother to move to since the Judge had promised the children back if she found a home and "lived decent." The real fears that the mother must have had that she could not live up to the court's demands were never mentioned and the worker "left thinking that Mrs. C. was pleased with the arrangements and happy to have such a nice home for her children." The next day Mrs. C. extricated herself from the dilemma by packing up and moving to another state.

Empathy is learned through listening and through striving to understand and to discipline one's own feelings. It is not easily acquired nor easily used. In fact it has been questioned whether the exhausting nature of welfare work is not to some extent due to the emotional strain that empathy requires.

CHAPTER VI

NOT DISARMING THE CLIENT

WE NOTED in the case of the unmarried mother discussed in the last chapter that when Jane would not talk:

> Worker commented on what a fine baby she had and that she would like to meet her other boy. Jane smiled for the first time and seemed very proud of the baby. Conversation was about baby for a while and during this worker felt a small amount of contact was made.

Nevertheless nothing significant happened in Jane.

It is possible that this attention and praise helped Jane come a little nearer, although not near enough, to the point where she could move. Certainly the worker intended it this way. It was meant to give some respect and encouragement to Jane as a person and to reassure her that the worker was not criticizing her for her immoral behavior. At the same time it is equally possible that this was what prevented Jane from making any movement at all.

How? There are two possibilities. It is possible that what Jane really needed to do was to express her rejection of this baby, to pour out her feelings about having him, about his father, about her feelings of guilt. If this was so—and we really don't know—then the worker effectually prevented her from doing this by making it clear that the "good" thing to do was to love it. Or again, perhaps what Jane needed to do was to "blow her top" about the welfare department, the worker and the whole sorry business. Sometimes people do move as a result of getting angry. We know this when we speak of a quarrel "clearing the air." Again, however, the worker's niceness made any such movement impossible.

In public welfare we seem to have become imbued with a concept that we must have a "good relationship" with our clients. This is fine as long as we mean by "good" a *constructive* relationship in which the client can grow and in which we do not retaliate on him for his mistakes. It does not make as much sense if what we mean by "good" is simply that client and worker like each other and get along fine.

This is, of course, the most comfortable kind of relationship to have. We do not like it if people get angry at us. We do not like it if they are unhappy about what we are trying to do for them. Welfare workers, I suspect, are particularly proud of their "good" relationships. They are, many of them, welfare workers *because* they "get along well" with people. (Child welfare workers are the most sensitive of all in this respect; a great deal of their satisfaction comes from being "loved by children and dogs.")

Our tendency is, then, to try to ward off expressions of anger or dissatisfaction, to praise or to flatter or to assure people that we like them when things become uncomfortable. This is what we mean by "disarming" a client. Webster defines "disarm" as to "deprive a person of his means of attack." It is exactly this that we sometimes do with clients.

Too much sweetness, too much sympathy, too quick a reassurance can disarm a client. We really don't know how a client needs to attack his problem but we do know that he must do it in his own way and if we don't let him feel as he wants to about it he may lose the chance to attack it.

This does not mean, of course, that we should not be nice to clients, that we should not extend to them every courtesy—one of the rather distressing things about the tape-recorded case whose beginning is given in the last chapter is that, although we know in this case that every word spoken has been recorded, there are none of those ordinary little courtesies that one expects in any contact, personal or professional, such as offering the client a chair, taking his coat or passing a remark or two on the weather. It doesn't mean, either, that we should not praise a client's baby or congratulate him on his child's grades, or anything that is sincerely meant to be just that—an appreciation of the client as a person. It does mean that we should be careful not to use this sort of thing to try to create something called a "good relationship" for its own sake, without considering what kind of a relationship the client can really use. For that is the trouble with a "good relationship." It is so often a substitute for the real kind of relationship the client needs, the relationship which comes from how we help him, what we do with him. So often, too, a "good relationship" is created because *we* want it to be this way, because *we* would like everything to be sweetness and light, because *we,* and not the client, are afraid of anything more real and perhaps more disturbing.

Clients, of course, use the same techniques on us. "I'm sure you'll understand, because you're such a kind lady." "My last worker never helped me at all, but you, now, Miss Smith, you're different." Knowing this should help us to see what we sometimes do in return.

Again, not disarming a client doesn't mean being hard, cold or indifferent. In actual fact it means just the opposite—letting one's empathy for the client recognize with him just how hard the situation really is. It is disarming the client with reassurance, kindness and facile suggestions that is actually much harder, much more cruel, because it denies the client's problem.

Let us look at how three workers handled a rejection in public assistance. The first is in the Farmer case. The worker's response to Mrs. Farmer is as follows:

I said it was hard to bring oneself to asking for help and then to find that the help one had asked for wasn't available without some pretty difficult conditions. I wondered what Mrs. Farmer wanted to do. Did she want to explore further whether we could help her in any other way? I did think that she was troubled about Eva Kate. Mrs. Farmer said that she'd have to manage by herself. I said that if she needed help, we would be glad to talk with her further. She left the room rather angrily.

This, as we know, led to movement. The second is in a case in which a change of agency policy rendered ineligible a woman who had previously been receiving APTD but in which the possible contribution of the son with whom she was living would now have to be taken into account.

The day following the mailing of the notice of rejection to Mrs. Wells she appeared at the office in a different mood than she had ever exhibited in any other contact with her. She demanded an explanation of the rejection of the application of the receptionist. When there was some delay in locating the record due to its being in the process of being filed and someone was preparing to talk with her in the absence of the worker, who had handled the case, Mrs. Wells would not be seated; she leaningly stood, shifting her overweight from one foot to the other. She snappily answered questions directed to her. Her face was red with anger and Mrs. Wells was about to explode.

When the worker took Mrs. Wells into the interview room she half sat on the chair offered her. She took the initiative in beginning the interview by explaining that she had proved that she wasn't able to work by her doctor's statement and by her employer's statement, that she had given the worker information that she had nothing in the world with which she could meet her needs. She said that her son and family made good wages but they had high rent to pay and other high expenses to meet. She knew many other people receiving help who were more able to work than she was at the present time and who had never worked as she had all her life since she was a mere child. She said she was so disappointed when she received her notice that she would not get help that she had to come and say what she thought about it. Worker told Mrs. Wells that we too were disappointed over the decision that had to be made regarding her application, that we are aware that she is a disabled person and that she has no income of her own with which to meet her needs.

Mrs. Wells interrupted to say well, why was my application rejected? Worker asked her if she had brought the notice of rejection with her and she said that she had not. Then worker explained to her the rejection on the basis of the preliminary budget showing her the figures of the budget and explaining to her the allowances which would be far below, probably, the allowances that they actually made and used, such as rent, the maximum allowance being $35.00 that we could allow in the budget when her son was actually paying $50.00 per month rent. Mrs. Wells was told that this is a new policy, one which the Welfare Dept. does not like either. We have been forced to use it because of lack of funds for this particular category and for this particular circumstance where the applicant lives in the home of a near relative. Mrs. Wells relaxed, sat back in her chair, and said to the worker, "Then if I move out of my son's home I will be eligible for that?" Worker said, "Mrs. Wells I cannot say that you would be eligible if you move; however, I will say that if there is any change of your circumstances in any way you may come to the office and make re-application and your application will be given every consideration."

Mrs. Wells then said, "Well I did not tell the worker but the reason that I want public assistance is so that I can get a place of my own, if only one room, to live separately from any of my children. I cannot bear the idea of being dependent upon them."

This record may be a little difficult for the worker who cannot allow that "independence" means to Mrs. Wells independence from her family, which, indeed, seems to have been the pattern of her life until the injury which first made her eligible for APTD. "Independence" to a welfare worker so often means only independence from public assistance. It is perfectly possible, in fact, that the state did not, or should not, intend that Mrs. Wells should have this privilege. Nevertheless, its policies certainly made this possible and to Mrs. Wells this kind of independence was very real.

Given the possibility of a difference of opinion here, about which I do not propose to argue, since it is irrelevant to the worker's handling of the rejection, what about this handling? I think we can see it as partly good and partly bad. Its value lies in the worker's statement that "we are aware that she is a disabled person and that she has no income of her own with which to meet her needs" with its implied empathy. Added to this is the worker's patient acceptance of Mrs. Wells's anger. Its weakness lies in the worker's need to disassociate her feeling, and that of the local agency, from the policy of the state. The worker isn't quite able to say, as perhaps she should, "I know that this policy may seem hard to you, but this is the policy of the agency at this time." She has to say, in effect, "I am on your side against the nasty old policy." This she has no right to do, nor is it really helpful since it may prevent her in future from helping Mrs. Wells with agency policies. Nevertheless, on the whole I think she has been helpful.

In the third case a grant to a family has to be terminated, since the stepfather of the four older children and father of the four younger is now physically able to work. Moreover the mother's former common-law husband has at last been located in another state.

On this date Mrs. Smith came by to see worker about their October check which they had not recieved. This check had been sent to our office until we could clear this case. We had talked with Mr. Smith a few days before this and suggested that he try to find a job since he is now able to work. We told Mrs. Smith that according to the doctor's statement her husband was able to work. Therefore, we will have to close their case. We also told her that since part of her children had two men responsible for them, she should be able to get support from them, and they are not eligible for help from this department. She said it had been twelve or thirteen years since Mr. Tom Jones had contributed to the children. She stated that the children do not hear from him, but he did come by to see them unexpectedly this summer.

She told us that Betty had gone back to work at Jack's Barbecue Place, but she had quit her job there last Friday and is trying to get a job somewhere else as a waitress. She also stated that Mr. Smith has been to the Employment Office twice and to some paint contractors, but he has not secured a job yet. Mrs. Smith also told us that the Power Company will turn off their electricity today.

Let us be clear that there is no question but that Mrs. Smith is ineligible. Technically the worker may feel that she has no further responsibility. But also let us consider the fact that Mrs. Smith is in a very serious situation. Her husband has not been able to find a job immediately; the chances of her obtaining support, at least in the near future, from a former common-law husband who has not contributed for twelve or thirteen years is very slight. Meanwhile the power company will cut off her electricity this very day. Yet, unlike Mrs. Wells, she does not get angry, or, unlike Mrs. Farmer, she does not suddenly resolve to manage this herself. It is true that she does ask the worker for her former common-law husband's address and says that she will write him, but this seems to be a rather inadequate response to such a pressing situation. One can't but help feel that she is "sitting down" under the weight of her circumstances.

It is possible, of course, that this is all that she could do—that no amount of struggling on her part, or resolution to go and see Mr. Jones, or plan to go to work herself, or whatever is open to her, would do any good. It is possible that she simply isn't that kind of person. Yet if there should be any way out, even a painful one, if there should be a spark somewhere in Mrs. Smith, the worker has effectually dampened it by her nice little totally unreal piece of "comforting"—"since part of her children had two men responsible for them, she should be able to get support for them." Is it unkind to suggest that here the worker was really unable to bear Mrs. Smith's despair if she really had to face the unlikelihood that this would be true and that therefore she had to pretend to herself that everything would be all right?

One of the areas in which we find it hardest not to be reassuring in almost a Pollyanna sort of way and one of the areas in which we are most apt to trade on a "good relationship" is in the placement of children. There may be good reasons for this. Some of us have never thought through how tremendous an experience it is for a child to leave his own home and go to another. We don't realize that this often means to a child that the fear he has been fighting all his life—the fear that his parents don't love him or that he is so bad that no one can love him—is suddenly made horribly real by the fact that he is leaving his home. One social worker has described this feeling as "akin to death, carrying with it anger, despair, disillusionment and a deep sense of badness." Others of us don't realize that this can be so when the home is unlovely, neglectful or brutal, when in actual fact it is exactly these qualities in a home which make a child cling to it in a desperate attempt to prove that it isn't so. But many more of us know these things in our hearts, or would know them if we could only bear to believe them, but can't put this knowledge to use.

There are many reasons for this and many ways in which we deceive ourselves. We are being good to the child in finding him a nice home. We ourselves would far prefer to live in a nice, clean, loving foster home than in the stinking, hate-filled hovel in which we may have found him. We are angry with his parents for having let him down. We are able to convince ourselves that children don't feel these things as deeply as an adult would, especially if the child cannot put his feelings into words. But even more than this we cannot bear to see a child unhappy. Our whole human tendency is to be protective, reassuring, comforting to a child in distress, forgetting that this may be disarming someone who needs every weapon on which he can lay his hands.

This is illustrated by one case brought into class. Bob, who is twelve, had been in trouble in the Juvenile Court and was to be placed in a boarding home for the summer. When his boarding mother came for him he ran away to the welfare office—a nice indication that he needed help. However, he did not get it and ran away again, the worker finally finding him on the highroad.

Bob got into the car and immediately began crying. Case Worker began talking to him and asked him why he didn't want to go to a boarding home for the summer. Case Worker told him how nice the boarding home is and tried to reason with him. Case Worker reminded him that the Juvenile Court Judge had told him that he would have to go to Training School if he didn't stay out of trouble   Case Worker said that if he went back home and started running around with the same crowd of boys again that he would get into trouble and would probably have to go to Training School. Bob said he knew this, but he didn't want to go to the boarding home.

When we arrived at the boarding home, Bob was still crying and refused to get out of the car. Case Worker, Case Worker Supervisor, and Mrs. X., and some boys at the boarding home, tried to persuade Bob into getting out of the car and looking over the boarding home, but Bob was still crying and refused to get out of the car.

Finally Case Worker went to the car and told Bob that we were only trying to help him and that he should at least get out of the car and look over the place. Case Worker told him that he would not be forced to stay at the boarding home and could make up his own mind about staying. With this, Bob began to stop crying and asked Case Worker if "I can make up my own mind and won't be forced to stay." Case Worker assured him that we were not trying to force him into doing anything but that we were only interested in his welfare and that we wanted him to stay at the boarding home so that he wouldn't have to go to Training School.

Bob then got out of the car and the boys at the boarding home showed us over the farm. We went first to the barn and saw the pigs, calves, etc. Bob began to brighten up and seemed to be enjoying himself. Next we went to the pond.

We had to pass the house on the way to the pond and one of the boys went into the house and got his air rifle. Bob shot it some on the way to the pond and when we got to the pond, he began to shoot at small fish around the edge. He killed one or two which seemed to please him very much as no one else had been able to do this including Case Worker. We stayed at the pond for about forty-five minutes and returned to the house. (During all of our tour of the farm the boys were telling Bob of how much fun they had—fishing, swimming, etc.)

When we reached the house, Mrs. X. had a cold drink for each of us and we sat on the porch and drank the colas while we talked and shot the air rifle. Bob seemed to be enjoying himself a great deal.

The caseworker certainly worked hard enough to reassure Bob—yet he ran away again the same night and was finally sent to the Training School.

We do not know exactly what was troubling Bob—there are some indications in the record that he felt that he was so bad that Training School was what he had to have. But the reason that we don't know is in part that the caseworker had made it so clear to him, in his efforts to reassure him, that he could not talk about the other side of the picture, the difficulties of being in a boarding home, the fears he had about it. One might say that the worker could not help Bob with his ambivalence because he didn't, or couldn't, come to terms with Bob's despair, and all that Bob could then do was to run away.

I don't pretend that this is easy. I know of no harder test of a caseworker's self-discipline than the need to let a child face his unhappiness and come to terms with it. When one has in one's car a weeping, desolate little bit of humanity—and all child welfare workers have had one from time to time—the urge to comfort, to reassure is overwhelming and one feels like an ogre if one doesn't; until, that is, one can replace sympathy with that far more helpful quality we have named "empathy" and can bear to suffer with the child. If only one can say and mean, "Yes, I know that it hurts. Yes, I know that even though there will be nice things in your foster home, there will also be times when you feel that you cannot bear it and you will hate the foster mother and me and the agency and everyone else who worked out this plan for you. But I do want you to know that I will understand it when you feel like this and I will try to help you if I can." This is the test of the person who is really on the road to being a caseworker, who doesn't have to protect herself or be defensive about her work.

Defensiveness is, of course, another way in which we disarm clients. We argue, or we put the blame on someone else—the state office, or the county commissioners or the federal government. This is what the worker in the Wells case quoted above so nearly did. It is a way of arming ourselves and disarming our clients.

CHAPTER VII

AVOIDING SELF-INVOLVEMENT

It must be clear by now that the concepts which we are discussing are not in fact distinct concepts but are very much part of each other. Thus, when the worker in the neglect situation which we discussed in the chapter on "Empathy" recognized that his own coming was one of the problems that the mother had to face he was at one and the same time showing empathy and refraining from disarming his client, and when the worker, in the case of the little boy in foster care, was disarming Bob he was at the same time failing to understand his ambivalence. The concepts are, in fact, simply different ways in which we can look at our actions with clients, some of which may help some of us and some others.

This is true of the concept of "avoiding self-involvement" which could be quite properly thought of as a part of empathy, but which to some people seems clearer if it is given a different name.

By avoiding self-involvement I mean simply not taking sides, either with a client against the community, or with the community against a client, or with one side or the other in a family quarrel. The worker who has developed empathy will not take sides because his interest is centered on what the person he is talking to or trying to help is feeling, here and now. Taking sides comes from sympathy, not empathy.

This doesn't mean, of course, that the worker doesn't have feelings of her own or is not very clear in her own mind about what is right or wrong. We must all have such convictions for ourselves. It means, however, that we cannot be really helpful until we give each person a chance to express to us his real feelings and to move in his own way.

Perhaps the best example of not taking sides that we have considered so far is the worker's empathic response to Mrs. Farmer after she confesses the beating of her granddaughter. It would have been easy to point out to Mrs. Farmer that beating the child would do no good—a fact which, in any case, Mrs. Farmer had discovered. It would have been easy, too, to make it clear that the worker's sympathies were with the beaten child and not the beating grandmother. However, if the worker had done this—and I don't doubt that these were actually her feelings—it would have felt to Mrs. Farmer as if the worker was only one more person who was against her. Notice, however, that the worker was not on Mrs. Farmer's side, either. Only a few lines further down in the case record she makes it clear that if Mrs. Farmer wants her to talk to Eva Kate the worker will have to work *with* the child and not *for* Mrs. Farmer:

I couldn't take over Mrs. Farmer's job of disciplining her granddaughter. Mrs. Farmer nodded. That meant that I couldn't be used as a punishment. Eva Kate would have to trust me, and that would mean that she'd have to be sure that she could tell me how she felt in confidence. I emphasized the last words. Mrs. Farmer said, "You mean you would not tell me." I said that I couldn't promise to tell her all that Eva Kate said, and Eva Kate would need to know it, just as she would have to know that I wouldn't permit her to tell me of plans that would be really dangerous to her, such as running away, without letting Mrs. Farmer know. But I'd have to let her tell me about how she felt about Mrs. Farmer, if I was to be of any help. Mrs. Farmer sat in silence. Then with a wry little smile she said, "That was quite a licking I gave her."

The worker in the following case has got into trouble because she cannot actually keep out of a family quarrel—in this case understandably, since she is trying to help two clients at once.

The client in this situation is a mother of two boys whose father has left them to be supported by the mother's father. She has herself applied for ADC.

Worker visited the home of Davis Kelly to discuss the possibility of Margaret McDuff's receiving assistance for two children, Don and Pattie.

Davis Kelly, the father of applicant, Margaret McDuff, has been regularly employed for a number of years with the Transport Company and was quite proud of the fact that he has been able to support his large family without having to ask for help from anyone, and was resentful that his son-in-law, Melvin McDuff, has deserted his family without having any apparent concern for them. Mr. Kelly said that he had supported the two children, ages ten and eight, for about a year and a half, and that he feels that Margaret and Melvin should feel more responsibility and act in their place as parents. Mr. Kelly went on to say that this was not the first time that he had had trouble with Margaret and that it all started just before World War II was over. A that time Margaret was going to Public School and was reported to

Juvenile Court for being truant, and upon investigation, it was found that she was carousing around with Melvin, who was then stationed in a nearby Army Camp. Mr. Kelly felt that the Court did nothing beneficial in their counseling and working with Margaret. He said that they spent all their time investigating his own background as a father and accusing him of being too stern and rigid in his methods of disciplining. He further stated that he had been and was a church-going man and that he believed everybody should be, and that he had only wanted to know who Margaret was going with and that he had expected her to get home at a reasonable time at night. In spite of his objections, Melvin and Margaret married. Continuing his condemnation of Melvin, he said that when the youngest child, Pattie, was born he had to go to the hospital and make the arrangements for her admittance, etc., and that Melvin was too busy gambling and drinking to be concerned with his wife. Margaret's condition at the time was considered critical and a number of donors for blood transfusions had to be secured. All this fell upon Davis Kelly, and he said that he felt that he had done enough.

Mr. Kelly's feelings are quite understandable, and if the worker had been able to see him alone she might have helped him with them, although not by championing Margaret. Unfortunately, however, Margaret is present.

Margaret cried intermittently during the investigation and said that her father was too hard on her, and we thought that probably she felt that her father was too insistent that she assume the responsibility for keeping Don and Pattie. Margaret does not find the idea of trying to secure work in this locality too appealing, for she said that she went to New York during the earlier months of the year and that the wages there were much higher. She considers fifteen dollars weekly an inadequate wage, and she could get a job making that much in the City of Athensville. She will not even consider working at that rate.

Mr. Kelly said that he would be willing to allow Margaret to remain in the home, although it was crowded, if she would pay a reasonable amount of her earnings. He thinks that she should reconsider going to work herself and should try to find a job. During this visit it seemed evident that there was a strong feeling of hostility between Margaret and her father, and she was pretty much opposed to anything that he might agree to.

At this point the worker turns to Margaret to ask her what she would really like to do about her family. Yet how quickly she actually denies her her plan:

She said that she wanted to go to New York and carry Don and Pattie with her, although she did not have any definite assurance as to work or any ideas as to where she and the children might live. Mr. Kelly said that this did not seem like such a good idea and that if Margaret wanted to go to New York alone and get work, he would keep the children if she would promise to send money for their maintenance. Mr. Kelly continued and said that he knew something about Margaret's promises and that sometimes they did not mean much. It seems that she had telephoned him several times while she was in New York asking for money when she was supposed to have a good job.

We told Margaret that we would help her work through this plan if she decided upon this since it seemed agreeable with Mr. Kelly, and that his wishes should be considered since he had been making a home for the two children. We further told her that we could write the Welfare Department in the area in which she planned to live and make arrangements for payments to be sent through the agencies.

Margaret, not surprisingly, counters this plan with action. She gets in touch with her husband and goes off with him alone, deserting both of her children. If only the worker could have seen Margaret alone and recognized her as the one who would have to make the decisions. As it was, all Margaret could see was the worker aligned with her father.

Avoiding self-involvement can also mean not being involved with a plan, with something either the community or the worker wants for the family or thinks would be good for them. As such self-involvement acts to deny clients the chance to come to terms with their ambivalence. One might even say that the reason so many of our clients do not really make use of our services is that we want them to do so much. The more we press on one side the more their ambivalence rises. Of course, they sometimes give in, go through the motions, but, as we pointed out before, so often such activity is self-defeating.

Watch how the worker in this case is so involved in what she believes are Alvin's rights that she does not give Mr. Brooks the chance to do any moving on his own. (This is one of the "canned" cases in which we saw the worker earlier trying to get Alvin back into school.)

Mr. Brooks in the office. The worker said that she understood that Mr. Brooks had not been able to work for some time. Mr. Brooks launched immediately into a long description of what he called "his misery." He has pains in the back and an unrepaired hernia. The only work he can do is logging and this involves carrying heavy weights. Worker asked Mr. Brooks if he wanted to get well, and Mr. Brooks agreed that he did. Worker asked if Mr. Brooks would go to our doctor if we paid for it, and Mr. Brooks said that he guessed so, only it wasn't so easy to get there. Worker said she would be glad to carry him and added that if the doctor thought that Mr. Brooks was sick, or if he thought that it would take a good deal of time before he could get well, we would be glad to take an application for ADC from him so that he would have a little money until he could get well again.

Mr. Brooks said that the family had money at this time. Alvin was earning between $30.00 and $40.00 a week and was bringing nearly all of it home. Worker said she understood that Mrs. Brooks was in need of medical care, and Mr. Brooks said that that was what the doctor said. Alvin had taken her to the doctor only the day before. The doctor had said that she needed feeding up, and this had worried Alvin who hadn't been making "that kind of money."

Worker asked whether Mr. Brooks wasn't worried, too. Mr. Brooks admitted that he was. Worker then tried to get Mr. Brooks to see that Alvin was undertaking responsibility which was properly Mr. Brooks's. Mr. Brooks made several excuses about being unable to work, etc. Worker asked Mr. Brooks if he did not want Alvin to grow up an educated man. Nearly every good job nowadays demanded high school education. Mr. Brooks didn't see how they would manage if Alvin stopped working now. Worker said that if Mr. Brooks could be helped to get well, he could support his family. If he was sick, the DPW could help for a while. It was not fair on Alvin to deprive him of his opportunities to earn a good living later on, and she was sure Mr. Brooks would not want this to happen. Mr. Brooks said he didn't know what Alvin would do, but he (Mr. Brooks) would be glad of a little help.

All one can say is—the poor man! His very thoughts are being thought for him. The worker is not stopping to listen to him. She is completely involved in her plan for Alvin. Compare this with the answer of a worker in the neglect case we have mentioned from time to time. Here the mother of the badly malnourished child is, for the moment, considering the possibility of foster care. The worker could well be forgiven if she jumped at this possibility for Patsy, at least until the mother could get on her feet:

Mrs. H. seemed much relaxed and spoke of her love for Patsy and her worry about the illness. The doctor has said that she ought to have orange juice, and they simply cannot afford it. She is quite terrified that Patsy will grow up to be a cripple. She again spoke of her difficulties, but her tone was quite different. Finally she said, "What would you suggest I do?"

I said I couldn't suggest anything; what had she thought of as possible ways out of the present situation? Perhaps we could think these through together. She said, well, she could place Patsy. She asked a number of questions about foster homes which I answered to the best of my ability—about visiting, whether she could be sure of getting the child back, about the standards of our homes. Finally she said, "I would really be Patsy's mother just the same, wouldn't I? She wouldn't grow away from me?" I said I thought she ought to realize that it wouldn't be quite the same during placement or even after it, that Patsy would make new attachments and that she would have to give up something of her mother's rights if she placed her. There would be advantages too in Patsy's having good medical care and diet immediately and in giving Mrs. H. time to get on her feet. Would she want to think more seriously about it? She said, "It would break my heart; Patsy needs me. Maybe I am not a good mother, but I am the only one she has got. No, that isn't the way. I know what I really should do, but I can't do it."

This brings up the question of what one does say when the client seems to ask us to make decisions for him or to express our views. In the case just quoted the mother, just before the passage we have reproduced, challenges the worker to say that foster care would be best for Patsy. The worker's answer is that he did not see any reason for suggesting that Patsy and the mother should be separated unless the mother saw this as a way out; after all, he hardly knew them as yet. His wisdom in not offering advice becomes clear as the mother, almost immediately following the discussion of placement quoted above, makes up her mind to get the help she really needs with her finances and with her marital problem and the case ends, as far as its neglect aspects are involved, on a triumphant note:

Patsy came into the room at that moment, a blonde, thin child who did not look too well, but had a lot of happy expressions. Mrs. H. scooped her up, saying, "Patsy, you are going to get well."

Family Service Society reported later that Mrs. H. had come in the next day after my talk to them and, though wanting some relief, had been interested at once in getting help for her marital difficulty. They thought that she could make use of their counselling service.

Similarly in the Farmer case the worker is faced with Mrs. Farmer's direct request to commit herself.

Mrs. Farmer said, "I think she's seeing her mother. That's what I'm afraid of. It wasn't true what I told you. Evie Belle did have TB but she's been out for a year or more. They tell me she's in town." She turned on me, suddenly a little angry. "You think I ought to let her see Eva Kate, don't you?" I said that I'd have no way of saying yes or no to that. All I could say at the moment was that Mrs. Farmer didn't seem sure that she could be a complete mother to Eva Kate. Eva Kate wouldn't let her, nor would Mr. Farmer, and Mrs. F. was reaching out for someone to take over some or all of the job.

In each case the worker is not ready to answer, but is ready to relate the client's question to her own feeling. This does not mean that clients do not occasionally need, and ask for, advice on small matters, but, when what they want is for the worker to carry the responsibility for a decision that must be theirs alone, the worker cannot allow herself to take this on.

CHAPTER VIII

PURPOSIVENESS

ONE OF THE differences between a social conversation and a professional one is that a social conversation has no particular purpose. It may have a sort of general purpose—to get acquainted, to spend a pleasant evening, even to impress a neighbor with how hospitable, or clever, or friendly one is. A professional interview has, however, a definite purpose, which is to come to grips with some part of a client's problem. Nothing is more meaningless than an interview that has all sorts of purposes, or none at all, or is just for the purpose of getting acquainted, or even making a "good" relationship.

In many cases the purpose of the interview is determined by the client. He comes into the office to ask for public assistance, or to tell the worker something, or to present a new problem. Sometimes, however, he is not sure what his purpose is and the worker has to help him define it, and sometimes the purpose has to be the worker's, as in neglect or juvenile court cases or where the worker must review a grant. Often the purpose is a shared one, or becomes so during an interview.

Two factors really govern the purpose of an interview. One is the actual nature of the service or services which the client and caseworker are discussing or are involved in. Thus an interview that is being held to discuss public assistance will have a very different emphasis than one that is occasioned by child neglect or by probation. The other is the fact that only so much can be accomplished in one interview. A person can usually take only one step at a time. Like a climber climbing a mountain, he may reach one level spot and need to rest there a little time before he tackles the next slope. If the caseworker tries to make him go further he may be so tired or careless that he slips.

Similarly, a person cannot be expected to take steps in all directions at once, nor can he be expected, for instance, to cut down a tree until he has cleared the underbrush away from beneath it. He can't be expected to use a service until he understands what it is about or until he can resolve some of his ambivalence about using it at all. All this calls for clarity on the caseworker's part about what the service he is offering entails and at what place in the process of using it he and the client really are.

Something of what may have to happen and what the caseworker may have to help happen can perhaps be understood if we consider that people are very complicated things, with all sorts of needs, some of them possibly contradictory but all of them somehow connected. This incredibly complex creature then comes into a little room to talk to a worker who at best has only a number of partial services to give and some of these perhaps rather inadequate. How are the two of them going to work together? How are they going to get anything done?

One way in which they might do this is to tackle a little bit of the problem at a time. This does not mean that the client is thought to have only one little problem, or that doing something about this little bit will solve the whole. But it does mean that by singling out some part of a problem to work with the client may he helped to get some courage about this bit and then have courage to tackle his wider problem. Possibly the outstanding example of this among the cases considered here is that of the malnourished child that we have quoted. In this case the mother, for some reason, could not bring herself to get either financial help or counselling help for her problem with her husband. She was ambivalent, confused. Possibly she could not ask even for financial help because this would mean bringing out all her problems about her husband. She was approached by a worker whose purpose (some people call it "function") was to see that something was done about the child. The worker did not believe that a lack of money was the sole problem or that if the mother could bring herself to ask for money all her problems would disappear. But he concentrated on helping her take this first step. In doing so he actually helped her to two things. She actually took the step of applying for relief and this was a tremendous victory. Perhaps more important still, however, was that she found out that people wanted to help her, that they were really interested in her. It wasn't that the worker said that he was interested. He didn't praise her or establish a "good relationship" by itself. It was not his charm or his friendliness that gave her this feeling. He actually showed that he understood her situation and that other workers would understand, too. Just before she scooped up Patsy to tell her that she would get well she said, "You know, when you came, my heart went into my boots. I thought you were going to take Patsy away. I didn't believe you when you said you wanted to help. I do now."

The worker did not at this time go into the marital difficulty. It was neither the focus of his service nor was she ready to talk on this level. Similarly, another worker interviewing a neglecting mother had to keep to his purpose, although in this case it was the mother who tried to keep away from it. He has just detailed to the mother the complaints made about her child's care, including the lack of warmth and food, Jo Ann's illness, etc.

Pearl said, "She's not seriously ill. I took her to the doctor. He says all she needs is warmth and food." The worker asked if she would get it and Pearl broke into violent denunciation of her husband. He was spending his money on another girl. He was never home. She had done her best. He was a low-down sonofabitch—and she did mean bitch, meaning her mother-in-law. She strode up and down the room, bare-footed, unkempt, dirty-faced and very angry. The worker said it must be hard to have to bear this alone. She stopped in mid-sentence and burst into tears. She loved her husband, but this other girl—. The worker said, "And meanwhile Jo Ann suffers." Pearl looked up, tear-stained, and said, "Will you talk to him?" An appointment was made for 4:00 that afternoon.

Two things should be noted here. The first is that twice the worker brings Pearl (the mother) back to the purpose of their interview—Jo Ann's condition—once when Pearl is bent on justifying herself and once when she is expressing her feeling about her husband. The second is that the interview ends when its primary purpose is reached, when Pearl, who ten minutes before was suspicious and antagonistic, can both ask for help and involve her husband in planning for their child.

Sometimes, and I think partly because our public welfare programs have undertaken so many different kinds of helping services, we confuse clients by having so much to offer. This does not mean, of course, that we should not have these things to offer, but simply that it puts an extra responsibility on us to know what our purpose should be at any one time. Let us look at a family which the worker described in handing in the case as a "family with multiple problems." She describes the family as follows:

Mr. Harold Hump—Age 41, small stature, meticulously clean, quiet and reserved in all contacts with Agency.
Mrs. Hump—Age 35, aggressive, resourceful, rather attractive in appearance and prone to exaggerate.
Betty—Age 9, very thin, resembles father and has "nervous spells."
Bob—Age 6, very thin, resembles father and has asthma.
Grandmother—Age 67, complainer, critical of Mr. Hump, resourceful and dependable with children.

This family group lives in a small mill village and all the residents are renters. Many problems have developed in this family over a period of five years. Medical care treatment for alcoholism and all types of non-financial services have been given this family group upon the request of Mrs. Hump as she is quite alert to the public services available and does not lack initiative. When Mr. Hump became completely unable to provide any financial help to his family, ADC was offered to supplement Mrs. Hump's earnings, and Mr. Hump was approved for APTD. All this time the family has had services through the Out-Patient Clinics at Baptist and Memorial Hospitals. The emotional problems of all members get beyond their control at intervals and they rid themselves of their hostilities, seemingly by word slashings, body beatings, etc. After their emotions are calmed, they start worrying about their financial needs.

Mr. Hump at the time of this interview has been going through a period of convalescing from a very serious heart attack. Mrs. Hump has given up her work to care for Mr. Hump and for the children, and her most recent request was for free school lunches.

Mrs. Hump comes into the office and starts off with a question about the school lunch problem. She then begins to tell the worker about her husband's behavior that morning—he had beaten Bob unmercifully and tried to choke Mrs. Hump. There is some discussion of Mr. Hump's needs and of Mrs. Hump's belief that he should go to a private mental hospital—a belief that is partially contradicted by Mrs. Hump's complaint that the Heart Association cannot work out a plan for Mr. Hump to work at home without planning on him keeping parakeets, which would aggravate Bob's asthma. The interview ends as follows:

Mrs. Hump, we realize that you have many problems and we sympathize with you but we are limited in our services as we have explained many times but we believe that this situation can be worked out with the cooperation of all your family. We will continue to do what we can for you. First, how would you like to talk with Dr. A. about your situation and see what he has to suggest, then we will try to go on from there. Mrs. Hump left the office somewhat calmer than when she arrived, but not with too much enthusiasm, stating that she would talk with Dr. A. and would ask him to call us.

It might seem at first sight as if the worker had helped Mrs. Hump concentrate on one part of her problem. Actually, I think, this wasn't so. All she did was to respond to one more of Mrs. Hump's problems, and her words suggest that this is really how she felt. One cannot doubt that Mrs. Hump has a serious problem. Her husband may even be insane. But she has one unrecognized problem on which she needs to work before she can really begin to work on the others. That problem is in herself. She needs to make up her mind whether she actually wants to do anything about any of her problems other than refer them to the welfare department. She needs to decide whether or not, for instance, she wants to go on living with Mr. Hump. As it is, she is trying to meet her problems piecemeal and on far too broad a front.

Again the worker in the Farmer case may provide us with a contrast. Although clearly Mrs. Farmer's primary need was not for public assistance, and although the agency undoubtedly had at its command all sorts of other services which it might have offered Mrs. Farmer, the worker kept the focus of the interview on the public assistance request until this was disposed of. Later, when Mrs. Farmer came back so troubled about her problem and asking for help in sending the child to Girl's Industrial School the worker again helps her to focus her problem.

I asked if Mrs. Farmer was still thinking of GIS as one way out of the difficulty. Mrs. Farmer said she had thought of it. A neighbor's daughter had been sent there but she didn't think it had done her much good. She came back as brassy as she was when she left. Besides she was sure her husband wouldn't hear of such a plan. He had strong feelings about his duty to Eva Kate, though he wasn't willing to take a hand in her discipline. I said that that made it even harder. Mrs. Farmer seemed to have to handle this pretty much alone. I also thought it was a pretty big decision. Perhaps all we could do today was to get over the next hurdle—what Mrs. Farmer would do if Eva Kate were late again. Mrs. F. seemed to have rejected both ignoring her behavior and beating her again. Mrs. F. said, "I could tell her I would send her to GIS, but that wouldn't be true. Could I tell her you'd talk with her?"

Purposiveness, of course, requires a clear understanding of a service and what it can offer. One worker brought into class a probation interview which she had had to handle without any very clear idea of what this service was. The girl, a fourteen-year-old who had had an illegitmate child who died, has been sent home pending her admission to the State Training School, but also with the understanding that if the father wanted to work out a boarding school plan he could. The worker dictates:

After cancelling two appointments, one because, according to Mary Belle, her father had not left her bus fare, and the other because she was not feeling well, Mary Belle came to the office. Counselor explained to Mary Belle that a routine physical examination was necessary before she would be admitted to the training school. Counselor explained to Mary Belle what she could expect in that examination. Counselor and Mary Belle talked of what she had been doing since the hearing. Mary Belle did not seem to want to talk about what she had been doing and made a statement that she had mostly stayed around home. Counselor wondered how her family had accepted the Court's decision. Mary Belle replied that she didn't know but they hadn't said anything to her. Mary Belle was asked if her father had written to the school he had been planning to write to, and Mary Belle again said she didn't know. Mary Belle was asked how her father had acted toward her since the hearing. Mary Belle replied that he didn't say anything at all. Counselor wondered whether or not Mary Belle knew whether her father had paid any of the damages as the Court had asked him to do. Mary Belle said that she hadn't talked with him about this.

Counselor inquired whether Mary Belle had mentioned to any of her friends or neighbors that she might be going to training school. Mary Belle said that she had not said anything except to one or two friends because the people in the neighborhood were talking about her. Counselor asked if Mary Belle felt that they did not approve of what she had done. Mary Belle stated that they thought she was bad because she had a baby but her friends didn't think she was so terrible. Counselor asked Mary Belle if she were dating. Mary Belle said yes. Counselor said she wondered if it were her same boy friend. Mary Belle abruptly said no, it was a different boy.

Counselor asked Mary Belle whether she thought she would like the new school which she would be attending in a few days in the neighborhood. Mary Belle stated she wondered if it was worthwhile to start school when she didn't know if she would be going to training school or not in a short time. Counselor explained to Mary Belle that while we were waiting to learn if her father could make arrangements for her to go to a private school, her conduct at home and in school might possibly be brought to the attention of the Judge who could withold the commitment as long as she was doing well. Counselor asked Mary Belle what she thought she should do to show that she was interested in staying at home. Mary Belle stated she supposed she should come in early and not run around so much.

Counselor then asked Mary Belle if she had any questions concerning the training school. Mary Belle said she didn't. Counselor went ahead anyway to tell her briefly what it was like. As counselor was leaving she reminded Mary Belle that part of the decision as to whether she would go on to training school was in her hands, and that the counselor hoped that she would continue to come in early although we were not telling her she could not go out but we wanted her to behave as normally as possible. At this point Mary Belle stated she did want to go out some and that she had a new boy friend.

The interview clearly wanders. The worker wants to know what Mary Belle has been doing, what her friends think, what her father plans. She tries to prepare her for a physical examination which she may not need. She finally gets around to what might be helpful—letting Mary Belle know that she has a choice. But then what does she do? She is representing the court which will have to make the decision about Mary Belle's behavior, or so it would seem from the conversation, although the prior material suggests that this depended on the father's planning. But she will not tell Mary Belle what it is that the court demands of her.

The whole nature of probation or of any so-called authoritative service is that it sets up a limited kind of choice. As a service what it can do is to help someone explore whether he can keep the law or not. No one can find this out unless he knows what the law is. Mary Belle could have been helped to come to terms with, or reject, certain conditions through which she might have got a grip on herself, and this would have been a purposeful service. As it was she was left vague as to what she might do.

The upshot, which may or may not be attributable to this vagueness but was certainly not prevented by it, followed five days later.

Mary Belle's father called the counselor and stated that Mary Belle had run away from home. He stated he did not know where she was but he wanted the "Court to look for her and take her to training school right away before she did any more damage he had to pay for."

This may not be everyone's idea of a probation service. Indeed, when in class I asked what might have been the purpose of this interview which seemed to have so many purposes, several of the class suggested that it should have been focussed on why Mary Belle had become delinquent. This would certainly have been a possibility, providing that the knowledge so gained was complete and accurate enough to be useful and provided that it was then going to be put to good purpose. I make this point because it seems to me that a number of public welfare workers have somehow got hold of the idea that knowledge about a client is valuable for its own sake.

But knowledge must have a purpose. In this case there could have been two purposes in gathering knowledge. The first could have been to help the judge decide more wisely for Mary Belle or to help the superintendent of the Training School provide the kind of treatment that would help her most. This would be valuable if the judge or the superintendent really had enough knowledge and knew what to do with it. The second purpose could be to help Mary Belle understand her own motivations and so change in some way. This again needs rather complete and accurate knowledge and, since the motivations of an unmarried mother are usually rather complex, it might be wise to have a psychiatrist to help one.

In any case, however, the purpose of the interview cannot finally be to find out why Mary Belle became a delinquent. It must be, in one way or another, to extend help to her so that she can stop being a delinquent.

Knowledge in itself, in the caseworker's mind or in the court summary, does not help with movement. It can only do so as it is used.

One might point out, too, that there are two kinds of knowledge one can use. One is the knowledge of Mary Belle as she was in the past and is now and is likely to be in the future. I wouldn't want to shortchange this kind of knowledge, properly used. I think it is always valuable to have. But there is also another kind of knowledge that we can have about Mary Belle, which has been largely stressed in this material. This is the knowledge of what Mary Belle, or any client, does with what the caseworker can do to help her—how she reacts to the service that is offered and its conditions, and what courage and resolution she can find in this process. This means looking at her as she works right here, in this interview, on this date, in this agency, in an interview set up for this purpose, and with this caseworker. It seems to me that sometimes we forget that this is really what happens between us and our clients—that we sit down and talk and struggle with what the client is feeling right here and now. And if we forget this we miss out on what is perhaps our greatest opportunity to help.

CHAPTER IX

WHAT IT MEANS TO BE A
CASEWORKER

GRADUALLY WE have been building up a picture of what a good case-worker is and does. I hope the picture is not discouraging—that it will be a real challenge and not some ideal that is impossible for anyone to try to approach. No one, I might say, can be a good caseworker all the time. All of us are much too human. We have good days and bad days. We can go so far and no further. We have a tendency in ourselves that we find hard to control which stops our being of help in some kinds of situations.

The point is, I think, that we should not be content with our failures. We shouldn't shrug them off and pretend that they don't matter. They do, rather badly sometimes. It is, I think, a valuable exercise for case-workers to sit down sometimes and really try to figure out how helpful they are. Perhaps this booklet will help provide a framework for doing this. Can I show real empathy for clients, or do I slip into being merely sympathetic? Even more important, am I better able to do this than I was a year ago? Do I disarm my clients to protect myself? Am I able to understand ambivalence even when it isn't obvious on the surface? Do I get involved either in my feelings for people or in plans for them that aren't really helpful to them in their problems? Do I see and appreciate movement even if it isn't the movement I would want to take myself? Can I use a service or an interview purposively?

I warn you that such a self-examination is neither easy nor always pleasant to undertake. It's very easy to kid oneself or to be blind about what is really happening. Nor will such an examination give you all the answers about your work. It is, however, worth the effort if undertaken honestly, and one can learn a lot from it.

Another way to look at this question is to consider the qualities of a good caseworker. They may seem rather frightening, but for what they are worth these are what I can see that he needs:

He needs self-discipline. This is perhaps the one single quality that distinguishes the good caseworker from the person who has all the right quality-traits but who has not yet learned to be a caseworker. That is what makes it possible for us to talk about a "professionally trained" caseworker. Some of what a "trained" caseworker has is knowledge. Obviously there are things to be learned about people and about services which can be taught in the classroom. But the core of professional training is the student's struggle to attain the kind of self-discipline that won't allow him to disarm clients, that will keep him clear of involvement, that will allow him to replace sympathy with empathy. This he does partly by trying himself out in a so-called "field work" experience, where his emphasis is not so much on the work he is doing as the testing out of his self-discipline with the help of a teacher-supervisor. This is the best way we know of at present to tackle the problem, but those who cannot spare the one or, preferably, two years that this demands are not absolved from the task of trying to develop as much as they can of this self-discipline themselves or with the help of their supervisors. Nor is it gained once and for all in a Graduate School. All good caseworkers work on it all the time.

He needs a special kind of liking and warmth for people. Just to "like people" is not enough, although of course, casework would be intolerable if one didn't. The "liking," however, has to have in it a respect for the other fellow, a desire to be of help to him but not to manage him or protect him, or necessarily to get along well with him or be liked by him. As I look back on the casework I have done as a child-welfare worker I find that I have probably been least successful with the group I "get along best with" and "like" the most—children from nine to eleven. That doesn't mean that I cannot be helpful to them as a Sunday School teacher, a camp counsellor, a father or a playmate. It does mean that I have to discipline myself to be a caseworker for them, because I find it hard to let them struggle with their real problems and even hate me if they have to. I want to protect them and have them like me.

Sometimes this special kind of liking doesn't go with being outgoing or popular. It may be found in someone who is quite shy or retiring.

He needs patience. So many of the mistakes we make are due to our impatience, our impulsiveness, our desire to get something done here and now that feels good. In situations which stir us emotionally we are particularly liable to be hasty. For instance, if a child has been neglected for a year it is really more sensible to let him go on being neglected for another two weeks while we work out plans that can be really helpful to him and to his family than to make a hurried, inadequate and sometimes disastrous plan the moment we find out about the neglect. Yet so often this is exactly what we do. I am reminded of a study one agency made of "emergencies." It was found that the incidence of emergencies was twice as high during dictation hours than it was at any other time of the day. In other words an emergency is often simply nothing more than something we would rather be doing than what we are doing at the time.

He needs courage. Casework is not a "sissy" activity. A caseworker needs real courage in allowing his clients to find their own way to a solution of their problems. He needs real courage to reject a client firmly, without apology and in such a way that the client can make use of the rejection. He may at times have to face a client with a very unpleasant truth—as, for instance, that a mother is neglecting her child or that if a delinquent does not do something about himself before he reaches the end of juvenile court age he will find himself in jail. The caseworker must brave anger, fear, sorrow and despair because these are the real things in the situation. At the same time he cannot protect himself because it is his client's and not his own problem that he is there to help with.

He needs imagination. He needs to be able to know what it would be like to undergo experiences which hopefully he would never face himself.

He needs knowledge. There may be some disagreement about what kind of knowledge, and how much, he needs, but there is knowledge that he can acquire. Certainly some of this must be knowledge of people. This book has made use of certain bits of knowledge about people—the fact that people are ambivalent about everything they do, the fact that the father of an illegitimate child is sometimes very unreal to the mother, the fact that children of unloving parents often cling more closely to them than do the children of loving parents. But there also has to be knowledge about the services with which one is entrusted, how they work, when they work, the principles behind them and what they feel like to use. One needs to know, for instance, that the mainspring of a public assistance program is the client's right to assistance if he is found eligible, and lack of this right if he is not, just as one needs to know that institutional care is not a service to offer to small children or to children who are long-time dependents without families, although it may be valuable for the teen-ager who finds satisfaction in a group. One needs to know in what way a counselling service differs from advice-giving and how one can use time to help clients come to a decision. One needs to know that the basic structure of a foster home program calls for a clear understanding of the respective roles of parent, foster parent and agency, or that the helpfulness of a juvenile court lies not in its willingness to do what the caseworker thinks it ought to do but in its ability to lay down legal limits to behavior in an understanding and non-punitive way. This kind of knowledge has not been stressed too heavily in this material, not because it is unimportant but because welfare departments administer so many different programs and under so many different conditions that to impart anything like a sufficiency of this kind of knowledge would require a much longer book.

And finally, *the caseworker needs faith*. He needs to believe that there is a purpose in life, that human beings, however confused or troubled or unhappy, do have within them somewhere, however deeply buried, the possibility of change, of movement. In fact the better the caseworker is, the more he will be surprised that even the most unlikely person is capable of being helped, that despite inadequate budgets, inadequate resources and our own inadequacies there is a source of help that we have called casework.

All this may look rather overwhelming. When we add to these qualities the ordinary ones of good organization, carefulness, integrity, ability to work with others, humor, good health, common sense and the ability to find one's way successfully down muddy lanes without stalling the car—all of which are important— we have a paragon who would be truly frightening in his perfection and who would be able to command five times the salary he gets. We can only do our best.

Fortunately, however, a caseworker does not stand alone. In fact it is one of the characteristics of a caseworker that he cannot stand alone. Casework, as we have defined it, is the way in which a service is given and this service has usually been determined by someone or something other than the caseworker—by the agency as it responds to public opinion and the convictions of its administrators, as it is empowered to offer services by the legislature or the county commissioners. While a good caseworker can make even an inadequate or a confused program be of some use to clients and a poor caseworker can nullify the helpfulness of even the most adequate and best thought-out of services, real helpfulness comes when a good agency employs good caseworkers to make its services effective.

Administratively an agency can do much to make the caseworker's job more fruitful. It can back up its services with adequate resources. It can be clear about its policies and procedures, so that caseworker and client know what it is that the agency can do and what it can't. It can work things out so that the caseworker is not so overburdened with either case-load or detail that he cannot find time to think about what he is doing. It can provide supervision that goes beyond checking up on the worker's work and gives him someone from whom he can get help in developing the skills and self-discipline which will enable him to achieve a real help-fulness. It can provide him with opportunities to learn either within the agency or in courses such as this or, if he can make use of it, in residence at a School of Social Work. The State Departments of both North and South Carolina have shown their quality in this respect in the way that they have publicized a course on which this material is based and made it possible for workers to attend it.

Of course one's agency may not have been able to do all these things to make one's service truly effective. Agencies are limited by lack of money, lack of trained staff, lack of public understanding. At times what an agency has to give may seem very limited or its restrictions harmful rather than helpful. Workers may feel frustrated in their efforts to be of help. This does not, however, relieve the worker of the responsibility of being as helpful as he can under the circumstances.

Particularly, present inadequacies in program, which are often simply "growing pains," are not excuses for poor casework. That is especially true of one of the public welfare workers' most frequent and, in a way, most justifiable complaints: "I don't have time to do good casework." Of course, a worker with a caseload of two or three or four hundred does not have time to do all that he might like to do to help his clients. Of course, he does not have time to engage with all of his clients in a very complicated or extensive service. But that again is not what we mean by "good casework."

There is, in fact, an answer to this complaint. It may sound like a hard one. It is, as a matter of fact, hard for many a caseworker to accept be-cause it deprives him of one of his pet illusions and because it demands of him an expenditure in self-discipline that is not easy at all. The answer that I offer you, with all that I can muster myself of empathy for the worker caught in the conflicting demands of applicants, reviews, statistical reports and deadlines and with full recognition that I myself have many times "cut corners" or failed to give what I should have in an interivew, is nothing more or less than this: a purposeful, empathic, non-disarming and non-self-involved interview today may remove the necessity for three, ten or fifty interviews in the time to come. It may even in itself be shorter as well as much more helpful. Good casework, in fact, takes less time than bad.

CHAPTER X

STRUCTURING THE COURSE:
A CHAPTER FOR TEACHERS

ON OCTOBER 12, 1955, as a result of requests from the Mecklenburg Chapter of the National Association of Social Workers to the School of Social Work at the University of North Carolina I found myself face-to-face with forty public welfare workers and committed to teach them "Social Casework I" for one and a half hours of graduate credit in the Extension Division of the University. These workers were of all ages from their early twenties to their sixties. Their experience ranged from two or three months to nearly twenty years; only in the kind of job they had to do and in the fact that, with a couple of minor exceptions, none of them had had any profesisonal graduate training were they a homogeneous group. The states of North and South Carolina were about equally represented; in all, workers from thirteen counties within a seventy-five-mile radius of Charlotte, North Carolina, attended the twelve two-hour sessions.

Obviously, such a course called for something rather different from what would be offered to beginning students on the campus. On the campus one has, usually, a small group—not more than twelve or fifteen in a class—not at the moment carrying direct casework responsibility, engaged in a two-year learning experience of which this is the very beginning and being fortified simultaneously by the offerings of other teachers. This was, however, a large group. Its membership was actively engaged in a job situation in the midst of which this course was a little oasis. The greater part of the class would, for various reasons, not be able to go into a full-time learning situation, and the course would have to stand by itself, not only in time but in its isolation from other teaching. This is not to depreciate what these workers might gain from individual supervision or staff-development projects in their states or counties but simply to say that this was something different. On the other hand, this course started with one great advantage. This was not just one course of many attended because "all first-year students take Casework I"; it was "the" course for which these workers had paid individually and for which they were willing to take both office and personal time and in many cases drive many miles in the dark.

I can claim nothing original for its structure. It was born of necessity and out of the ideas of my colleagues whom I would probably have consulted in any case but did especially since Social Casework I is not my usual assignment, which is Child Welfare and Public Welfare Administration. My first reaction was to want to split the course, to teach it in two or three sections or to involve other teachers, but this proved administratively impossible. I wanted to teach it as it was taught on campus. I had not considered its difference. Gradually, however, I came to terms with its particular demands and I think that what we tried worked.

The first requirement of the course was that each student bring in to the second meeting a disguised interview from his own caseload. This should either show what the student thought was movement on the part of the client—we had discussed this in the first meeting in relation to one of the "canned" cases—or should be a situation in which there had not been movement and in which the student wanted help. The latter type predominated.

Of the forty-one interviews submitted—one worker added a tape-recording of an interview he had conducted that morning—nineteen were selected for class discussion. There was some loss, of course, in not using twenty-two interviews in which workers had invested time and effort, but this seemed inevitable. These cases were returned with the instructor's comments. In general, these were cases in which there was insufficient evidence to show or even to speculate intelligently why movement had or had not taken place.

The selection and arrangement of the nineteen chosen cases took some thought. Eventually they fell into some sort of progression—frequently in pairs showing contrasting activity or attitude—through which the instructor could raise successively certain fundamental questions. This does not mean that we considered ambivalence, for instance, only in relation to cases E and F, but that E and F were chosen to illustrate the concept of ambivalence which had first come to light, say, in case C and also, perhaps, to begin discussion on a concept that would be high-lighted by cases G and H. Also, in general, cases in which public assistance was the primary service were grouped in the early part of the course since the majority of cases submitted were in this area and since the group's concept of casework at first allowed for little skill in administering this function.

However, by the end of the course the group had considered cases in which the primary service was probation, a protective service, foster care placement and, in one case, counselling to a family who, in the words of the student, "presented multiple problems."

These nineteen cases became the main subject matter of the course. Each week two interviews were assigned to the class as a whole for discussion the next week. Specifically, however, five members of the class were appointed a special panel to bring in written notes and to begin discussion of the case. This they would do until each member of the panel had responded to at least one of the leading questions asked and until the flood of questions and observations by the other class-members could be held back no longer.

The so-called "leading questions" were appended to the mimeographed interview. For instance, one pair of cases contrasted a client who became angry over rejection and from this forged for herself a new resolution and a case in which the worker had hastily "disarmed" a rejected client by a show of sympathy and a number of specious alternatives. The questions appended to the second case read as follows:

Compare this case with the Wells case (Case E).
Why do you think Mrs. Smith did not become angry as Mrs. Wells did? Did the caseworker have anything to do with this?
Realistically do you believe that Mrs. Smith can get support from her family? If you think not, then what is unrealistic, if anything, about (a) the agency's policy, (b) the caseworker's handling of the case?
How might this rejection have been handled more helpfully for Mrs. Smith?

On the whole, rather more unsuccessful than successful cases were used, although in three cases, at least, the casework was of a very high order. The authorship of the cases was not disclosed but in more than one instance the worker involved claimed the case publicly during the discussion even when the class's criticism was forthright.

The panel method meant that each worker, with the exception of five who were "spared" or gave up their turn in order to provide a final "summary" session, was responsible for at least two definite contributions to the general discussion and had, in addition, the experience of analyzing consciously the work done in two cases. It was the experience of the instructor that panel members took their responsibility very seriously. In addition, in several counties, cases used in class were re-discussed in staff development meetings with workers who had not attended the course.

Students were also asked for three pieces of written material, as follows:

1. *A personal experience in asking for and receiving help,* due the

third week of the course. This was designed to help workers identify both the defenses of the person asking for help and the importance of certain attitudes on the part of the helping person. The general implication of the papers was discussed in class but each paper was responded to individually in writing. A very large proportion of the workers could identify their own difficulty in asking for help and their own ambivalence towards the helping person and this helped to identify the same feelings in clients. It was perhaps significant that the majority of instances cited involved asking for money either as a business loan or from relatives. Next came asking for a job and getting help with stalled cars!

2. *A reading report* on a rather minimum amount of reading, due after six sessions. This was phrased as follows:

Read *one or more* (preferably at least two) of the following and comment on in terms of the following questions:

Is the material helpful to you in understanding the nature of casework?

Do you agree with the writer? Where do you differ from him?

What seem to you the most important ideas he puts forward?

What would happen to you and your clients if you put some of these ideas into practice?

There was a real administrative problem here as most of the students had little or no access to libraries. Books and periodicals had to be brought in rather limited quantities from the University Library at Chapel Hill. Ten different pieces of material were brought, some in multiple copies, varying in length from sixteen to seventy-two pages, and on the basis of cards signed each student averaged reading between four and five of these. The most helpful were probably Herbert Aptekar's *Basic Concepts in Social Case Work*, Chapters I through V, and Chapter V of Arthur Fink, Everett Wilson and Merrill Conover's *Field of Social Work*, 1955 edition. The class were not, however, ready for the last question in the assignment at this point in the course, tending to see all their problems as solved if these ideas became used and not seeing their own difficulties in using them. The main value in the reading was to provide a more consistent conceptual base than the class discussion could offer.

3. *A final paper evaluating the student's own progress as a caseworker* in terms of the concepts developed in class, some of which were listed. This paper, which carried 30 per cent of the grade for the course, was, if the initial sentence of a vast majority of the papers is to be believed, very difficult for most of the students to undertake. Many said that they had never been asked to do anything like this before, but very nobly they responded to the challenge and very real, in many cases, was their recognition of their difficulties in self-discipline, their understanding of

their past mistakes and their justifiable hopes for the future. There were two most encouraging features about these papers. One was the conviction expressed in some of them that the writer's effectiveness as a caseworker had actually increased during the course and that he was being more helpful to clients in January than he had been in October. The other was that most of the writers recognized that this was only a beginning, that there was still much to be done. In a number of cases the student hoped to go on to full professional training, in others he knew that he must go on alone but felt that he could still improve.

As a second part to this paper students were asked to discuss one case presented to the class and to identify what they learned from the discussion. It was good to know that so meaningful and so potentially helpful is any case record that each one of the nineteen cases presented was chosen by at least one student as having been the most helpful to him.